THE ZEN OF ART

The Zen of Art

With Notes on the Art of Life

Carolyn Schlam

Shanti Arts Publishing
Brunswick, Maine

The Zen of Art: With Notes on the Art of life

Published by Shanti Arts Publishing

Designed by Shanti Arts Designs

Shanti Arts LLC
193 Hillside Road
Brunswick, Maine 04011
shantiarts.com

Printed in the United States of America

ISBN: 978-1-962082-21-1 (softcover)

Library of Congress Control Number: 2024934257

This book is dedicated to my dear sister Eleanor Toby.
I only wish she were here so I could read it to her
and make her proud. I send her my love as I try to wrap
my arms around her with my words. I am holding her hand.

"The main thing is to be moved, to love,
to hope, to tremble, to live."

—Auguste Rodin

Contents

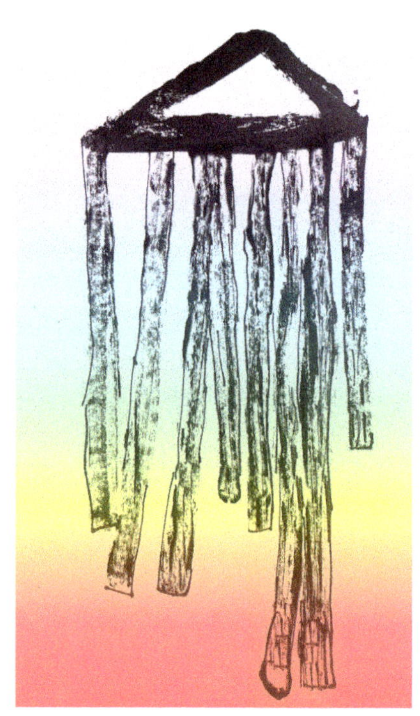

Wing Song, Charcoal drawing with digital enhancement, 12 x 9 inches

PROLOGUE

Wind Song

I am sitting on my front porch in a rocking chair. It is a gloriously sunny February day in southern California as spring makes its debut. I am drinking coffee with my dog lying beside me. We are the picture of contentment, and I am feeling blessed to have the sun on my face and this place to dream. There is a slight wind, and in my relaxed state, I become aware of the tinkling of wind chimes.

I have two sets of chimes: one large, with an alto voice; and the other is tiny and strikes a high treble tone. I ordered the smaller of these from a catalog and was dismayed when a dramatically smaller chime than I expected arrived in the mail. I had been fooled by the catalog photo. Now I am positively gleeful to discover the duet my two chimes are capable of offering.

As I listen this day, I hear the wind orchestrate my chimes into what clearly is a repetitive pattern, a melody, if you will, a song. The pattern has slight variations like my sheets of classical music, and I get quieter to notice the various elaborations of the theme.

Alas, there is no composer, no songwriter, lest you charge the wind with authorship. But the wind has no mind, no consciousness. It is itself—energy—yet today it is directing my chimes so I may delight in this morning concert.

I ponder this moment. It seems important, consequential. And when I think about it, I realize that Art—with a capital A—is created in much the same way as this impromptu piece of music. The only interference is the artist's self-consciousness inserting itself into the process. To do, yet get out of the way, is the way of the Zen of Art.

The source of creative initiation is like the wind—an impetus, inspiration, a force that moves, motivates, prompts, encourages the artist to begin. Like the chimes, it stirs the feelings, sensitivities, thoughts, mental and physical and spiritual being of the artist. And the result of this coupling is art.

The wind does not exert itself with intention—either forcefully or even tenderly. Neither does it direct or mold. Certainly it does not judge. It is just the chance meeting of source and instrument that results in the shape, tenor, touch, and meaning of the creation that is born.

Think likewise of the lone sperm swimming in a great sea of its kind, winning the lottery of life and piercing the egg. The result: a being that is a unique conglomerate of possibilities, carrying a new name. All it takes for the impetus we call nature to find its destiny—the instrument, artist, egg—is this process, and new life or art is made.

This in essence is what the Zen of Art is about—to recognize how our art and our lives are created; to revel in the naturalness of that process and to follow it where it leads; to let art and life happen; to know that we are steeped in nature, so letting it be is letting ourselves be, without disruption; to trust that the song will be written by the wind as it engages with the chimes. Let us dance with the wind to create visions, dreams, and beauty beyond knowing.

Remember the story of the wind and the chimes, the symbolic creative partnership that composes the symphony of existence, as you read the rest of this book. This story is its heart.

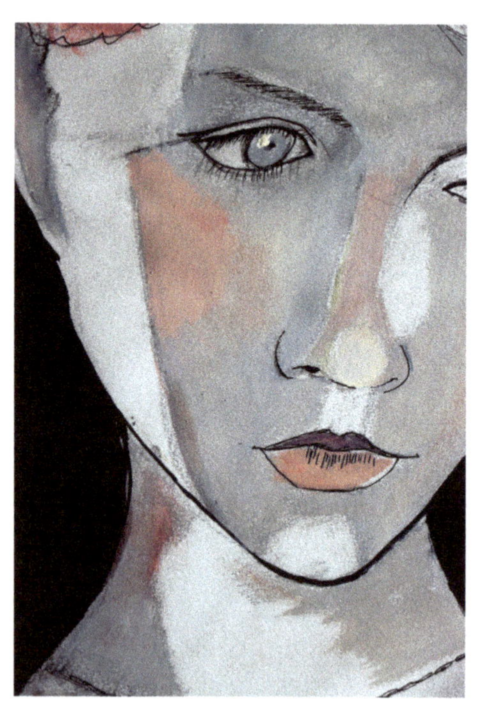

Heart, Pencil and watercolor, 19 x 24 inches

INTRODUCTION

Zen and the Creative Life

"We have what we need, if we use what we have."
—Edgar Cahn

I am an artist and a writer, a lover of imagery and language. I am embarking on this new adventure to offer you, through word and picture, some of what I have learned in this merry-go-round called life and through my practice of art. I am hoping that it will interest, inspire, and inform you, and above all, that you will find the spin enjoyable and worthwhile.

I am not a guru or a sage. I am an ordinary person who has endeavored, like you, to become mindful, to learn, and to grow as a person. I would call myself a seeker and an expressive. I have been searching for meaning, identity, wisdom, and love for all of my life. Through my art and my writing, I have also worked to express what moves me, what brings me joy, and what matters,

I have been interested in and inclined toward Zen, and what are labeled "new thought" ideas, since I was a teenager. I have read many books on the subject and have incorporated yoga and meditation in my daily life. But I am not an expert in Zen philosophy and practices in any sense of the word. I do not offer you Zen with a capital Z in any authoritative sense but rather my application of it to something I am much more familiar with—art.

As I pursued artmaking with many materials and in multiple

genres, my interest in philosophy and Eastern thought continued to percolate and then merge with art practice. The concepts are complex and may seem puzzling. They are difficult to hold in your mind as they run contrary to many assumptions and theories prevalent in modern life. But they have persisted, and I have now, after years of working as an artist and simultaneously pondering these ideas, decided to put them all together while making sense of what seems so perplexing, yet true.

So here it is—The Zen of Art.

Let's start with the words in our title: first, Zen. You may be familiar with Zen and know that it is connected with Buddhism, as in Zen Buddhism. Zen is a Japanese sect of Buddhism associated with meditation, intuition, and enlightenment.

Digging a little deeper into the derivation of the word "Zen," we find that it is a variation of the Chinese word *channa*, which, shortened to *chan*, means "meditation" or "contemplation." *Chan* is the transliteration of the Sanskrit *dhyanam*, meaning "to see, observe." The Indo-European root of this word is *dhya*, which simply means "to see." In Greek, *dhya* became *sa*, which is a "sign" or "distinguishing mark."

What does this all mean to us? The word "Zen" has become popularized today to mean more than the abbreviated name of a religion or spiritual practice. Zen today is a way of approaching life, an attitude, a philosophy that can be brought to bear in any context. You will find books with titles like: *The Zen of*. . . cooking, dancing, and the famous and wonderful *Zen and the Art of Motorcycle Maintenance* by Robert Pirsig, one of my favorite books. Then there is the classic *Zen in the Art of Archery*, a 1953 work by Eugen Herrigel. Zen is a "way" that can be applied to any activity. It is a way of thinking, seeing, being. A way to live. A way to love. A way to be present.

In this book we will apply this philosophy to the activity of making art. The *Oxford English Dictionary* provides us with this definition of art: "The expression or application of human creative skill and imagination, typically in a visual form such as painting or sculpture, producing works to be appreciated primarily for their beauty or emotional power." I've written a lot on what art is in previous books. Suffice it to say, for this purpose, that art is the practice of communicating thought and emotion in an expressive manner. A gross oversimplification, to be sure. But useful. When we put the two words together, as in *The Zen of Art*, I will be talking about what, how, and why to apply the Zen attitude and posture of contemplation, immediacy, and direct seeing to the practice of art.

Art has taught me how to live, and living has conversely taught me how to make art. I have probably made most of the mistakes and taken nearly all of the false steps that an artist is capable of, and I have watched students fall into the same traps. I have also found the escape hatches, windows, doors, vistas, and roads that lead to creative breakthrough, exhilaration, beauty, revelation, and joy that the practice and appreciation of art can provide.

A Zen koan is a story, dialogue, question, or statement that Zen Buddhists use to bring practitioners to realization. I will attempt in this book to give my modern non-sectarian version of the koan. I will offer anecdotes, questions, and illustrations, whatever I can think of to make these ideas clearer and more understandable. Some of these will relate to art practice, but many are just evocations of life experiences that we all share.

My hope is that you will find something here that you can relate to regardless of your profession. I believe that life is a canvas we are given, upon which each of us paints the story of our soul and our incarnation here on Earth. The colors are the experiences, happenings, and events that come to us and that we create. The medium is our philosophy, our attitudes that enable us to interpret these experiences in a unique way. The resulting painting is our life, a work of art. Every one of us is truly an artist as we endeavor to create ourselves and our lives.

So, fellow artists, I invite you to follow me down this particular pathway that I call *The Zen of Art*. Because a picture may indeed be worth a thousand words, I include images that may speak with more clarity than my verbal vocabulary. I have visioned the ideas in this book to be coupled with some of my artistic efforts, many of which are fragments or sections of larger works. In a sense, this book is a journal of my thoughts, happenings, and visual ideas.

As you will discern from these artistic excerpts, I am primarily a figurative artist, obsessed with depicting human beings, especially women, in many different configurations. Why did I concentrate on this subject? My eyes and brain are enchanted with the human form, and identity is a subject I gravitate to more than any other.

Veering from one's habits is a critical dynamic in growth, and assuredly, if not a Zen command, certainly an ethos. So I wanted to challenge myself artistically in some way in this book. Though I've concentrated on the figure in my painting and drawing, I have at times tackled other subjects, media, and stylistic interpretations. If I just stayed with the familiar, I could be accused of violating all the principles and attitudes I extol here, and that simply would not do. So in that spirit, I inaugurated some experiments in abstract painting to discuss here. The process and the images of the work I created are elaborated in the last chapter called "Studio Diary."

I have always found it unfortunate that when we view a work of art, we just get to see its final iteration, and this makes it seem that it arose like magic. The creative process—the back and forth, adding and subtracting, the seesaw until resolution is reached or exhaustion prevails—is hidden. We are not privy to the intense struggle that characterizes the making of works of art, and this leads to misleading ideas about the genius of the creator and the nature of art itself.

It's useful to see what did not work and to learn why. This is perhaps even more helpful than studying the remarkable pieces that seem to emerge full-blown, without effort.

So come along with me as we engage with these ideas and ask what Zen has to do with art, and how it all relates to the way we live and think about our lives. Delight, wisdom, and peace is what we are after. Let's take the first step.

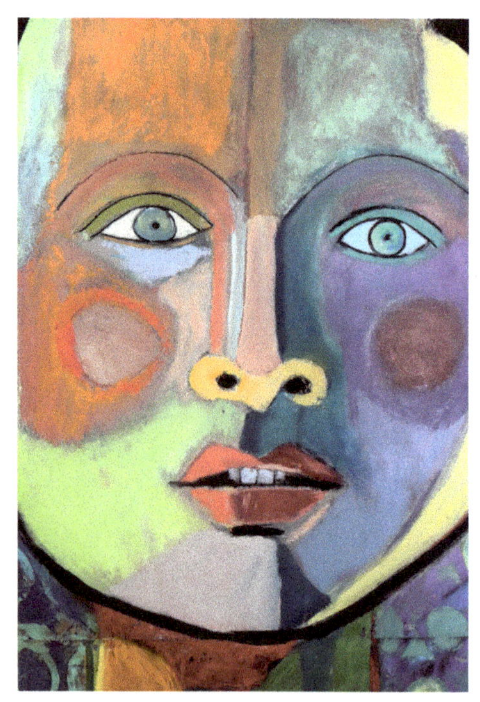

Girl, Oil on board

ONE

Awakening: The Beautiful Beginning

> "To be old can be glorious if one
> has not unlearned what it means to begin."
> —Martin Buber

Inspiration

Ah, the beginning. The glorious, enchanted beginning. Birth. Genesis. In the first moment there is unending, boundless possibility. Nothing has been uttered. No decisions have been made. No doors have been closed. We know this unconsciously and consider lingering here, feeling this hesitation to act, break the silence, begin.

So before we take the first step, make the first line, splash the first touch of color . . . before we go from nothingness to nonesuch, let us pause.

Take a breath.

In-spire. Take in breath.

Reside in the magnificent emptiness of zero, from which can emerge infinity. So before, breathe.

Know that once we move, touch, strike, draw, plunge, there is no turning back. We are on the road to evolution and will arrive at a final destination—karma. It is set, written, if not perhaps in the mind of the all-knowing, in the deeds themselves. Inevitability. Destiny.

Every artist knows this. That is why when we stand at the easel, brush in hand, we stop, wait, breathe before beginning. There is a push and pull—we can't wait to get started and also, simultaneously, we don't want to start because we don't want to leave the Garden, the bliss, the unhindered and yet unnamed potentiality. Infinity.

As humans, incarnated beings, we are charged to move, to live. "Movement is life," said my dance teacher Blanche Evan, and she was right. We know that starting takes us one step closer to the end, but we go anyway.

Some of us will rush headlong, passionately into our work. Others of us will hold back, go slowly, savoring every line and mark. Which is better?

Working with fever, rushing headlong has its benefits—we don't have time to think.

Working with calculated thought has its benefits—we proceed with care and love.

We instinctively know that all beauty lives in the beginning. Childhood. The first stirrings of a love affair. The plunge into the water.

Sunrise. From the quiet blackness into the glory. Light.

Making a piece of art is a journey. A journey that begins with the first breath of inspiration, which stirs the maker to begin, to make that first mark. When she makes that mark, she does not know her destination; it has not been revealed. Yet she imagines something—a supposed destination. She is going to . . . OK, France, and so she gets on a plane with a destination that says Paris. She knows it is summer so she has packed light clothes and made sure to bring a bathing suit. She has on her good walking shoes. Yes, all that . . .

But what France will turn out to be for her is totally unknown. Will she encounter an old French man on a train who will tell her the secret of a long life? Will she fall into the Seine? Will she meet the love of her life and buy him a balloon? Will she fall sick and lie moaning in her hotel room?

Just like the traveler, the artist has an intention for her creative trip, a longing to explore a particular place, some hopes and plans for what might happen, and a preconception of what that place is like. But she won't KNOW until she gets there. She will make it up as she goes along, one happening will lead to the next, and then she will be back on the plane, completed work of art in the suitcase.

This is the joy of art, consonant with the joy of life, the journey, going into the unknown. These trips are fascinating and memorable, most especially the occurrences, feelings, and thoughts we did not expect or plan. What do we tell our friends when we return from a trip? Surely nothing about the familiar sights we expected to see. No, we comment on the things we did not see coming—the guy with the balloon, the swim in the Seine.

As we become experienced travelers, we may become less adventurous, more programmed in our habits. So too, artists. If we've been very successful with the color red, we may be putting it everywhere, always returning to the same cafe, so to speak. We'll talk more about this later.

Right now, let's go back to the topic at hand—booking our tickets. Beginnings.

This takes me to a memory. My then husband and I used to plan a winter trip every year. In those days we used a travel agent. About a month before our proposed trip, we would hop down to the agent's office and pick up a stack of brochures elaborating all our vacation choices. We would take them home and pore over them for days, discussing the pros and cons and zeroing in on our favorites.

Now that I think back on it, I can honestly tell you that these days were often the best of our whole vacation. The anticipation was even better than the actual holiday. You can probably relate. Why do I tell you this?

I urge you to remember this when you make art: Stay a long time in the beginning. Linger there. Frolic around in the deliciousness of anticipation, imagining the places you may go before you map the route and plan the itinerary.

Know that in the beginning you are very close to your inspiration, you have all the time in the world to get to your destination, and it will serve you well to hang out in this realm of possibility. Don't rush to grow up, because when you are old, I guarantee you will wish you could play some more, loll about, take in the sights.

When we are children and we don't know what is wrong or even what is expected of us, how do we engage with our very new world? We play. We don't yet know what not to do, and this makes us free to experiment, improvise, explore. We make up stories, we invent characters, we imagine places, we move into myriad dimensions, unimpeded by rules, time, fears, even names and definitions. We play and we are as imaginative and unimpeded as we are ever going to be.

When we have grown and been introduced to all the nos and musn'ts and shoulds, we may have forgotten how we once played. We think it is now time to work. The conundrum: To work well as an artist, you must first play.

Every beginning allows you to be a child again. The newness of your effort exhorts you to return to this special time. Before you know where you are going, take in the view. Breathe.

Every new work begins with undefined, nameless play. Abstraction. No name. The big picture. Once recognition dawns and your route is set, if all goes well, play will morph into joyful work.

Childhood. Scientists claim it to be the most important period in a person's life. Why? This is when the tone is set, the basic shape and character of one's life is formed. The early choices show the way for all future development, and they govern irrevocably what is most likely to follow. Do you recall the 1986 book by Robert Fulghum titled *All I Really Needed to Know I Learned in Kindergarten*? He was onto something, wasn't he?

In the domain of artmaking, these early choices are about subject, size, direction, and placement. I have worked with many students and have observed them all make the same mistake: rushing headlong into making the semblance of an object and skipping over some crucial decisions. Instead of experimenting with the most desired size or placement, they rush to finish and ignore critical steps in the process that are crucial determinants in how the image will ultimately look.

The student's immense talent pushes them forward, but it is too soon. They wind up with a beautifully detailed image that is too small, misplaced, distorted, weak. They settled too soon, rushed too fast, didn't give the image a chance to sit, breathe, establish itself. The end came too fast, and there is no place to go, no place to grow.

It is a cliché but makes the point: glorious architecture is posited on a strong foundation. Before you can go lofty, you've got to get the math down. Otherwise, your building will simply not stand.

We do rush too fast to grow up—in life as well as art. And it does us no good. When we give ourselves time in the beginning, a good result is possible.

All of the choices we make are so important. We have our best chance when we make them mindfully, yes. But we are human, so sometimes that is not possible. We make a poor choice. What to do?

If you go astray, if you make a critical mistake, if the image is too small or in the wrong place, if you are working long hours and find you have strayed from your initial inspiration, or if your work has gone in a different direction than you intended and you are not happy with where you've landed, all is not lost. When things are not going well, *go back*. Go back to the beginning, to the happy place, the playground where all is possible and there are no regrets. Your new journey will be much more auspicious, I promise you.

Beset by false trails, mistakes, unfortunate efforts—you can return to reinvigorate. What is notable about beginnings is an openness to feeling and experience, the lack of preconceived or tired ideas. One of the words used to describe this Zen attitude in Japanese is ***datsuzoku***, a word that does not have an equivalent in English. It means something like "the willingness to experiment, to act unencumbered by formula." The closest analog in our language, I guess, is "originality," but the Japanese word is deeper and more complex.

Sometimes artists consider innovations in their work to be accidents, but this is not entirely accurate. Perhaps the words "unexpected" and "new" would be more descriptive and positive. With the mind and feelings set free, so-called accidents happen in art. *Daysuzuku* encourages artists to follow this path.

Take the long road and savor the view. Not just the obvious, the standouts. Note the weather, the light conditions, the tint of the hour. Do not hurry to define, name, classify, prettify, polish; all these take you quickly to the end. Yes, take the byways, but if you go so far that you are lost, retrace your steps back to the source and then venture out again.

The beautiful beginning—"tripping the light fantastic," a phrase that has come up repeatedly in literature and song since the time of Milton, originally referring to dancing in a gay and nimble fashion—is something artists do wax about. Robert Henri, author of *The Art Spirit* and a wonderful art teacher, called it "the butterfly of the imagination."

Close your eyes for a moment and imagine the *tripping* of that butterfly as it flutters, practically weightless, evanescent, lovely. I gave myself the assignment of painting that butterfly and recommend you give it a try as well. A daunting task, it was inspiring to the max. As I recommended in my book *The Creative Path*, taking on seemingly impossible tasks is a great way to keep oneself tethered to the beginning. How in the world can you be definitive about something like this?

Here's how I would describe artistic initiation. You see something or imagine it, and it gives off a ping. Let's say you are walking along a rustic path in summer and you notice that the ground has turned golden. The light is particularly lovely this time of the day. It is dusk. When you look up at the hills, they seem to glow in a purple light. You are enchanted, realizing how beautiful is this palette of gold and purple. You are stirred. Inspired. You want to share this beauty you have witnessed, you want to paint the dusk.

In the studio you lay out your paints. A yellow ocher, a blue, and a red, of course. But you know as a painter that these colors that have pleased you are part of a much bigger story. There is the ineffable color of the light that has made the glow. Other colors are needed as a foil. Textures and lines are necessary to express what you have seen. It is complex.

If you are smart you will stay wedded to what inspired you—the glow—and not get sidetracked making trees and rocks. Oh, the trees and rocks might eventually appear, but you will not make them. You will bathe in the glow, and the glow will make the trees and the rocks. Believing this will happen and letting it be so is the Zen way.

It is explained in the concept of *wu-wei*—non-interference, a creative process that is organic. Letting the seed develop into the tree of its own accord, not making the tree, just planting the seed with full confidence that it will not only develop but grow into what it is intended to be.

Inside the acorn seed—the inspiration—is the acorn tree—not the oak tree or maple. Every work of art is a tautology. From the inspiration comes the art, and it can only become itself. Let it be. Let it become. Do not interfere. Follow your own inspiration and stick with it. Let the art happen.

There is a rhythm to artmaking. In the beginning, we go fast. Ray Bradbury likens his process to a weather report: "Hot today, cool tomorrow." What he means is that in the beautiful beginning he is as free and unencumbered as can be—he's hot! There is plenty of time, if he has the inclination, to cool his story down—that is, edit it—but he knows that without the heat, there's no story at all.

Here's how the artist Joan Miro expressed this concept: "The works must be conceived by fire in the soul but executed with clinical coolness."

Remember, there will be a time to analyze, to break down what you have done, to rip it apart even, but that time is not now. Too much criticism is interference that will break the flow of creativity.

Instinctively, we know the way. Our inspiration gives us the *wu-wei* and shows us how to dance it out. The rhythm will be different for every artist. You will learn yours.

A sculpture made from a hollowed tree is an example of the rhythm of artmaking. How did it come about? The log was lying in the forest when I chanced by, not looking for anything in particular. A rotted piece of burned wood. Looking closer, it transformed before my eyes. No longer just a slab of wood, I saw a woman's torso. Once I spied this treasure, I was afraid someone else would discover her, so I pulled her into a safe spot. My fear was probably for naught; was it likely that someone strolling by would see this woman hiding in a log? My discovery secured, I ran home to get the hand truck and excitedly returned to retrieve her and bring her to the studio.

Then began the process of revelation, ripping the image out of the wood. A laborious, agonizing job, taking away the extraneous chips until, bit by bit, she emerged, sustained by my conviction that she was there all along. The artist as deliverer, facilitator, conduit. Just doing a job. No ego. I ripped and ripped, went home with sawdust on my clothes, shoes, and up my nose, but she was revealed. I dubbed her *Tree-She*.

When was I the artist? When I labored in the studio with my grinder ripping my art out of this intransigent piece of burned

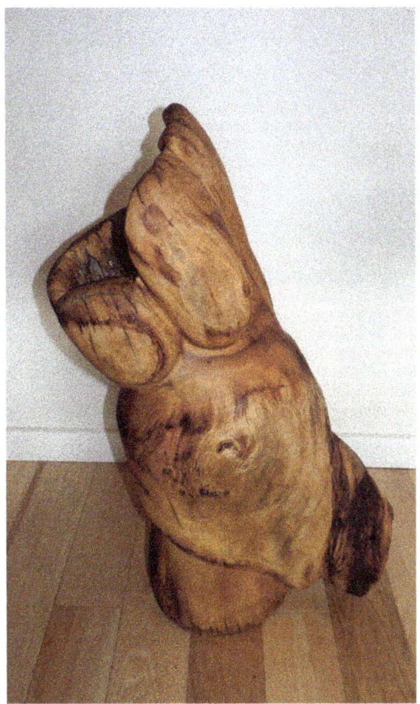

Tree She, 2017, Wood, 42 x 18 x 18 inches

wood *or* when I found her in the forest? The answer is obvious. The artist is the seer who receives the message, then manifests it so others may find it as well. Remember, we must wear those alert eyes so inspiration can be found. Taking that walk in the woods was an essential and perhaps the most important part of the artmaking process because therein was the visioning, the source.

Creative work requires a particularly open state of mind, a mind so open and welcoming that creative impulses are unimpeded by judgment. As they come to us, we are grateful, trusting. We follow them even if they are unfamiliar or contradict other impulses that have come to us in the past. We are wholly in this moment, without bias, accepting direction from our inner selves.

To summarize: Don't get in the way of your art. Let it lead. It knows the way before you do. Don't judge. Just do.

We follow these creative directives like a gleeful child following its mother on a path to a birthday party. What are we celebrating? The birth of a new piece of art.

Spontaneity

Art is a kind of magic, downright alchemy, isn't it? That Bach minuet is so perfect in its syncopation. That Matisse window so glorious. That Bradbury story so punchy. How did they do it? Are they illusionists, masters of the beyond? It certainly seems so.

It is marvelous, yes, but it isn't magic. It seems so because we don't see the steps; we just are amazed by the result. I can vouch for this. I have amazed myself with what I have managed to create. Did I make that? I wonder. How did I do it?

I am stepping up on the diving board. It's pretty high and the water looks far away. Can I do it? Make the leap? Just go for it? I put my arms over my head, and I leap up. I've done it. I am spontaneous.

Am I?

It feels great but let's just think about it. I have lived a while in my body, and I know what it is capable of. I have also calculated unconsciously the arc my body must make to land correctly in the deep end. I have learned that the water will slow my descent so my head does not hit the bottom of the pool. I'm taking the leap, but I have enough information to do it successfully.

Of course I could be wrong and miscalculate and hurt myself. But my experience has given me the confidence to try. I am courageous, perhaps, but not foolhardy. Spontaneity is not rooted in ignorance; it is a calculation based on trust, both in myself and in the forces of nature.

We want our art to be fresh, not staid, and we don't want our extreme effort to show. But that doesn't mean we don't have to work at it. In truth, it takes a whole lot of work to be spontaneous.

In Ray Bradbury's fine book *Zen in the Art of Writing*, he talks about his practice, telling us how he made lists of titles and put them in a mental bank only to be pulled out when inspiration struck and he could match an intention to an inspiration. He elaborates on how he honed his craft by writing a thousand words a day—rain or shine. A huge amount of thinking, planning, practicing, and steadfastness had to be invested before he could, as he describes it, sit down and in two hours write a terrific story. All that work so that when he climbed up on the diving board, he could take that leap, be spontaneous.

It's a lot easier to be spontaneous when your skills are top rate, and you've practiced. You know the answer to the old question: "How do you get to Carnegie Hall?" PRACTICE so you can be spontaneous. PRACTICE so you can be free. PRACTICE so you can soar.

In Zen thought and writing, many questions are asked. Here are a few. Can one intend or try to be spontaneous? Doesn't intention contradict spontaneity? Zen tells us that this duality between intention and spontaneity does not actually exist. In fact, all of our actions, both voluntary and automatic, arise naturally like breathing. Intention itself arises naturally and therefore is itself spontaneous.

Isn't this marvelous and liberating? It is foundational to Zen that we—our egos, our minds—are part of the flow of life, that there is no place to get to because we are already there. Trying to be spontaneous is silliness. We just have to be, to act, to get out of our own way. That is the way.

You have probably heard this familiar saying: "There is no road to peace. Peace is the way."

You may substitute any word you want for *peace*. It is also popular to say, "Don't try. Just do."

Both of these expressions argue for that noninterference we spoke about previously.

Our action plan does not release us from the need to study, prepare, and learn our craft. In fact, it does not, by its very nature, forbid any other activity you employ to make art. That would be a negation of the Zen way, which reveres diversity and individuality. Zen is orthodoxy turned on its head.

To live in the moment is to be spontaneous. Just remember, what you have experienced in prior moments is money in the bank. It has become part of the you that meets this moment. Spontaneously. Perhaps miraculously too.

Perception

To be ready to leap as an artist, you'll need courage, practice, and desire. You will also need to amplify your senses and learn to make extraordinary connections. It isn't sufficient to just function, to get by, to master all the regular skills humans need to live: things like looking where you are going, minding your Ps and Qs, being kind and considerate, and all the things you learned in kindergarten.

You need to ramp up your perception of the world around you, ramp it up so you notice things other people don't. Why, you ask? Because you are an expressive. That's your job—to express. And in order to express you need to pay such close attention to the world that you see things that are not necessarily visible to the naked eye, at least to the eyes of most everyone else. You see thing with your greedy, artistic eyes, and you connect those visions to something you want to say. That's how art is born.

Those greedy eyes of the artist are connected to his or her mind and heart in an entirely personal way. Other artists' eyes don't want the same things and will not find them. The eyes of an artist are projections of his feelings and, ultimately, his soul.

Expressiveness requires abstract thinking and the ability to connect something you sense or feel to something larger and more consequential. This is an essential component of artistic practice.

A painter drawing a model does not just see a foot. She sees the foot contextually and in an animated way. A contraction of that foot says pain or stress or sexual tension. So she doesn't draw a foot. She draws the sexual tension. This concentration changes the look of the foot and the viewer consequently feels something when she looks at the drawing. That is what makes the drawing expressive.

When the artist paints a portrait of a child, she is painting innocence, not merely a childish appearance. This informs all the notes and lines she makes on the canvas. When Rembrandt painted his own self-portrait as an older man, he was not interested in simply creating a reasonable resemblance. His colors, shapes, lines contain theories of mortality, poetic volumes on life and death, and are anything but arbitrary or descriptive. That is why you look at them with amazement. They speak—and reek—of emotion.

Whether or not what you see on the canvas is recognizable, the artist is always painting something more than the object itself. We might say the object is informed; some meaning has penetrated and changed it, meaning perhaps rooted in a quality, an idea, a mood . . . something. Youth. Love. Exuberance. Sorrow. Afternoon. The artist's notes are chosen with these intentions in mind. Verisimilitude to an object may be a blinding obsession, yet it simply does not suffice even if it is expert.

Look deeply into works of art that stir you, and you will find that they do not merely describe. They present something more than a facsimile, something unique and personal, something transformed.

You have doubtless heard the expression: "A picture is worth a thousand words." This is absolutely true. If you are deeply engaged with a work, you will find that you need many words to explain it to yourself or communicate what you see to another. The title is only a gateway to the deeper meaning.

Visual art is *charged* imagery. Even a photograph can be charged. The artist's or photographer's choices are what you are seeing, not the object portrayed. And those choices come from the psyche of the artist.

This dedication to the content beyond mere description is what makes art interesting and important. In striving to depict it, the artist transcends the physical. You can imagine how you would draw a hand. But how do you draw love? What colors do you use to paint grief? How do you add the smell of fish to your painting of one?

And this is where the magic enters the picture. The informed object cannot be copied. It must be conjured, and this requires a leap of imagination. How this is accomplished is original to each artist. It is also what makes the process so fascinating for the artist as witness.

Again, this is what distinguishes art from reportage. The artist is expressive and paints her subject not only the way it looks, but the way she wants it to be seen.

Think of Matisse's color-saturated treatment of the window and how it so beautifully captures the delicious light in the south of France. You can almost feel the sea air. Think of how Bradbury took his everyday experience and carried it to an entirely new planet of his making—Mars. Yes, there is a Mars, but it's surely not the one Ray conjured. Nor was Lin-Manuel Miranda's Hamilton anything like the actual historical figure.

You might argue that these artists got to the heart of their subjects and captured reality, but because they did it not by copying what was there but by re-creating it with inspired vision, let's say it becomes a *new reality*, a *new being.* This is possible because the artists' perceptions are enhanced, punctuated, and validated by individuality of feeling and thought.

It is okay to get by with perfunctory perception if all you want to do is get by in the world. But if you are a creative and an expressive, you are burning to make a new world. So you have to look hard, think deeply, be incredibly receptive so the pings from the universe can find you, zap you, sting you, puncture your heart, keep you up at night while you wait to get to the studio.

And they will find you. All you have to do is exercise and prepare to be amazed. When I say exercise, I mean doing an inordinate amount of looking, practicing, playing, noting, experimenting, and, yes, failing, falling short, messing up. Keep wanting to say something, to be smarter, braver, fresher, wilder, better.

When you do well, smile. When you do poorly, smile. Both actions are taking you to the next level and then the next. You are in the flow of artistic creation—you lucky person, you.

We can relate this passionate perception to the Zen focus on action, not self-examination, introspection, and self-recrimination, the latter which only stands in our way, prevents us from acting, and interferes with the process of creation. Zen compares the mind, as Alan Watts expresses it in *The Way of Zen*, to an eye that sees but cannot see itself. We find ourselves by looking out and are able to express our inner vision because of this heightened perception.

By the way, when people worry about artificial intelligence

making art, I shake my head in deep skepticism. This is partly because I doubt that practicing artists are the people designing these scary algorithms. Have they programmed in the ethereal, the evanescent, the improbables, the impossibles, the links we make that arise from our dreams? The artist's prompts are living in his unconscious and find their realization in private moments when no one is looking. I think those AI creatures can only scratch the surface, faking their way into making art. You need a soul to make art, and I don't think anyone has figured out yet how to invent one of those.

No-Mind

As the artist works, little by little she expands her vocabulary of art. Technically, for sure, as she becomes more and more competent, learning all the eccentricities of her tools and medium. Practice makes you . . . if not perfect (we'll get to that later), certainly more skilled, more knowledgeable. What is the point of all this?

There is a Zen concept referred to as *wu-shin* or *mushin*, which translated means "no mind." This is a confusing term because it suggests both a lack of something and also something impossible to conceive of. We undoubtedly have a mind—an ability to conceptualize—so what is this state of no-mind. Is it death?

The concept is often discussed in relation to the martial arts as a way to combat one's opponent. In this context, no-mind means the freedom from ego, anger, or fear in confrontation. The individual is certainly awake and his mind is functioning, but without intention or plan. He is free to act totally out of intuition, to be completely in the moment. This is the Zen *art of war*.

No-mind can mean "open mind," a relaxed state of complete immersion in the now where there is no judgment, no emotion, and no attachment to the outcome. How does this apply to art?

We hearken back to that diving board. Armed with knowledge

and experience from previous trials, the artist is sometimes able to achieve such a state of immersion in his work, with technique so internalized, that he is able to proceed seemingly automatically, without thought. Without mind. No-mind. Key to this state is the ability to just do and to forego judgment altogether. This is the equivalent of being in the proverbial *zone*—so in the moment that we are not trying to prove anything to ourselves or to others. This is the path to mastery in art, what we all hope for, and sometimes, if we can let go, do achieve.

We say the painting made itself. So what does that make us? We are witnesses, not makers; celebrants, not boasters; guests, not hosts.

The no-mind state does not come easily or often as we strive to create art. When it does come and we are so totally engaged that time has stopped, it seems to make all our efforts worthwhile. We have captured, snatched from life a taste of the divine. The art we have created seems so much more valuable and precious as it has been our ticket to this experience.

I have experienced *wu-shin* in the studio on many days when my concentration was fierce and I became oblivious to my surroundings or other concerns of the day. Most recently, I had such an afternoon in the making of a particular collage. My intention was to express the extreme tenderness of the mother and child theme, which I love and have returned to many times. My inspiration was strong, which is crucial in achieving this level of immersion. The greater your fascination with your subject, the more absorbed you can become in expressing it.

I started in early afternoon, drawing and cutting papers. Like in a dream, I continued working, not stopping or looking up for hours. How to express that connection between mother and child? How to draw joy on the mother's face? How to create shapes that say adorableness in the child? What patterns say tenderness? What are the softest of colors? Draw. Cut. Place. Move. On and on. Don't stop. When the light was gone, I looked down to see my vision realized. I loved it!

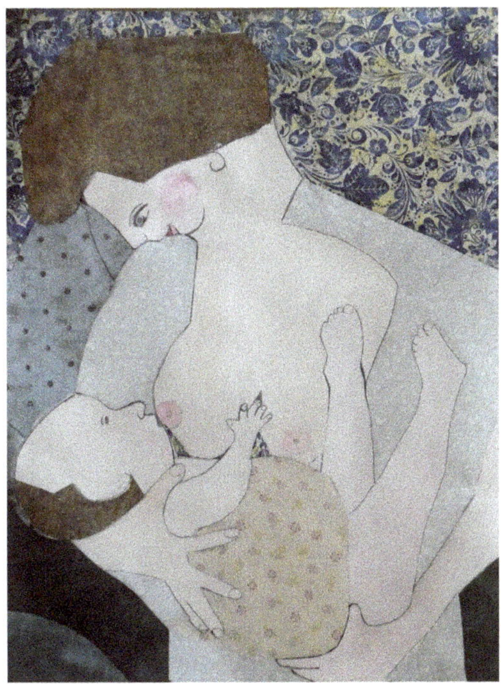

Mother and Child, 2021, Collage, 30 x 22 inches

Many artists describe their inspired sessions of artmaking as an experience of timelessness, such utter absorption in an activity that it feels much like a dream, outside of time and space. Indeed, that is one of the great rewards of making art; where there is no separation of self and other and such rapt attention that we disappear into our work, we become invisible in the making of it.

It was one of the most wonderful afternoons of my life. When it ended and I looked down at this piece of art, I was spent, but jubilant. I believe I experienced no-mind.

Alas, this beautiful state of no-mind cannot be ordered, demanded, or manufactured. It happens when we least expect it, at a time when our task is so important and consuming that our ego remains asleep. Though we cannot make it happen, we can recognize it when it does, and allow ourselves to feel the immense gratitude it evokes. What a privilege!

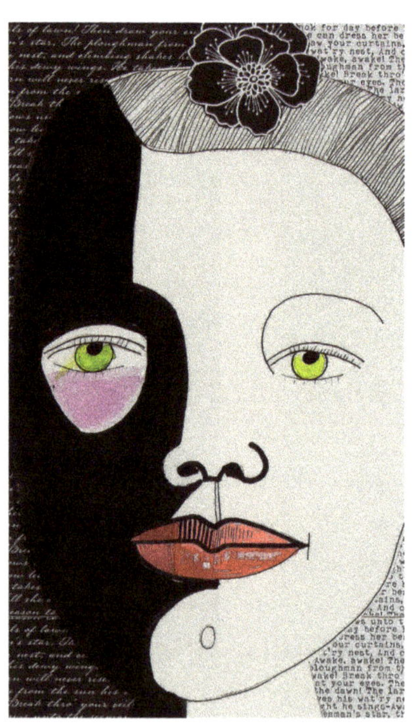

Herstory, Drawing, 24 x 18 inches

TWO

Simplicity

'Tis a gift to be simple, 'tis a gift to be free
'Tis a gift to come down where I ought to be
And when I am in the place just right
I will be in the valley of love and delight
When true simplicity is gained
To bow and to bend I will not be ashamed
To turn, to turn will be my delight
'Til by turning, turning, I come 'round right.

—Joseph Brackett

Words do deceive, as they are so liable to interpretation. Simplicity is a word that is associated with Zen, but let's dig deeper. Oxford defines it thusly: "The fact or quality of having a simple form, structure, design, composition, etc.; lack of complexity or intricacy."

Here are its synonyms: artlessness, candor, clarity, classicality, clean lines, directness, guilelessness, integrity, lack of adornment, modesty, purity, restraint, unity, chastity, clearness, ease, easiness, homogeneity, ingenuousness, innocence, monotony, naivety, naturalness, obviousness, openness, plainness, primitiveness, severity, singleness, straightforwardness, uniformity.

Some of these synonyms ring true, others seem to veer, at least from the Zen concept. Homogeneity and uniformity, for instance, seem limiting; monotony and severity connote judgment. Plainness and lack of subtlety rule out myriad works of art.

Classical too. I can think of many romantic works that I would also describe as emblematic of simplicity. So let's see what does fit.

One word missing from the list above is one that I associate with a successful art process, and that is distillation. Oxford tells us that "a distillation is the extraction of the essential meaning or most important aspects of something." Following that period of play we described in the previous chapter and marching toward realization of our vision, what exactly do we do? We add elements that support our intention, and we remove those that obfuscate. We distill.

Our frivolous play goads us to say more and more, and before we know it, our work has become a veritable kitchen sink of this and that. Distillation is the most wondrous plucking out of all the juicy tidbits that, despite our enthusiasm, do not make the grade. We jubilantly extract that detritus from the boundless sea of our creativity. How do we choose what to eliminate?

In my earlier book *The Creative Path*, I quoted my teacher Norman Raeben; his exhortation to his students was to "Say one thing but really say it." What he meant by this powerful phrase was to follow your inspiration so truly and completely that it is not only clear but also commanding. He recommended that we weed out anything that was extraneous, anything placed to conceal, prettify, or sully the kernel of truth—what he referred to as the "one thing." Not only were we to keep true to our mission, we were to have our work shout that mission to the nth degree—not to equivocate, but to "really say it." In other words, the focus is not, for example, on the quantity of details that are incorporated into a work; the focus is on truth—whether those details serve the essence of the work. I think this idea is in keeping with the Zen idea of simplicity.

Here is jazz musician Charles Mingus on the idea of simplicity: "Creativity is more than just being different. Anybody can play weird; that's easy. What's hard is to be as simple as Bach. Making the simple awesomely simple, that's creativity."

To speak simply, to express simply is then just this: to be true. But true to what? True to inspiration, true to vision, whatever it might be. It can be busy or quiet, loud or soft, fancy or plain, as long as it is just itself, no more, no less.

Clarity

I use the word *clarity* to discuss this idea of the singularity of notes within a work, not its quality or composition. One can achieve clarity in art in any genre, any treatment. A minimalist work may have no more clarity that a cacophonous one, as long as the latter is totally itself. It is clarity of intent and execution that define the work, not the emptiness of the canvas.

As an aside, I do believe that the movement of minimalism and the desire to eliminate the object and go completely abstract are driven by this desire to achieve clarity and to make art that is revelatory, not complicated and confusing. It often is described as an attempt to get down to essences by paring away distractions. Though the intention might have been noble, one must be careful not to go too far. It is not wise, as the expression goes, to *throw the baby out with the bath water*.

If the goal of art is expressiveness, this is the singular criteria. Do all of the marks, colors, textures advance that singularity of message? If they do, the work is successful, even masterful. This may be more difficult to achieve in a work with many patterns, layers, and images, but not impossible.

You may think I am lobbying here for a boring kind of art founded on consistency, sticking to a particular style or treatment. But I am not. I am hewing to my teacher's admonition to "say one thing." That means doing one thing in one work. But you can be boisterous in one work and positively sober and serene in another. That's okay, even recommended, as our moods are many and our creativity boundless.

One of the reasons we fail to achieve simplicity in a work is that we don't exactly know what we are going for. I won't say "don't know what we're doing" because that's not correct. We may be in the stage of the process I will call "hunt and peck," looking for notes, themes, and treatments that will work and *work together*. We're exploring. Our intention is still nascent—an artistic fetus, if you will. This means that we are open to receive; we are in improvisational mode. We may land on a tangent, a new direction that seems promising but was heretofore not in the soup at all. A byway that can become a tributary and take us into new territory that makes us forsake our former intention and hop onto a new vision. If this happens there's a lot we have to get rid of in the work. It might even be a big brush moment when we have to completely start anew.

When the road becomes clear, we are poised to achieve clarity. Clarity can be gained over time or in moments—clarity of inspiration, intention, and purpose. It is easier to achieve clarity in drawings done quickly from life as you are taking information from a source and getting it down before you have a chance to introduce contradictory notes; there's simply no time to get into trouble. You can run into considerable confusion with works made over many days as you are coming to the task in many different states of mind. I have often had the experience of looking at something I've done with praise on Monday only to find it totally lacking on Tuesday. Sometimes it is best to wait until Wednesday to move forward, leaving a day to empty your mind lest Thursday bring regret.

A koan-like representation of the difficulty achieving purity of purpose might be an apocryphal story about the impressionist Claude Monet, known as The Eye for his faithfulness in trying to paint the color of the light.

Any painter who has worked *en plein air* will tell you that light conditions are continually changing, and one would have to paint dozens of paintings to accurately document the exact color of the light. What the artist is actually doing is painting his memory of the light at 7:32 a.m. during the course of the several hours it might take him to paint it. By 7:40 a.m., the very dutiful and diligent Monet would have had to remix all those delicious color choices to faithfully represent them. Oh well, let's not get technical. Forget about absolutes and just enjoy the effort. After all, the truth is only an approximation. And you have to give Monet kudos for recalling those matching 7:32 a.m. color mixtures.

There is nothing limiting in this call for clarity. It can be achieved in any style, any manner. You might call it consistency, but that belittles the act, I think. Commitment is more positive and accurate. Commitment to your vision, whatever it may be. Commitment to produce work that has a clear message and is totally itself with little or no extraneous clutter.

Just an aside here. Though I am all for consistency in the context of a single work, I don't think an artist's body of work needs to sing the same tune or sing it in the same key, so to speak. I support and cheer artists who range far and experiment with technique, style, subject, and media in the course of their artistic practice. Without these forays and explorations, artists run the risk of simplification to the point of emptiness, where they are no longer engaged with their intention, but instead work automatically, their work becoming so rarefied it is no longer relevant. Relevancy is consonant with feeling, and repetition tends to tire us, and dampen enthusiasm. Doing something new brings our awareness back to life.

Authenticity

Authenticity is a much used word today. The determination is prized and called out as *speaking your truth*. Indeed nothing is more important in art than authenticity. Why is that? you ask.

If the purpose of art, it's very essence, is to *express* one's thoughts, feelings, and point of view, doing so without artifice and with purity of heart and intention, well, that's the whole game right there. Zen is very keen on this point, and there are several terms that elaborate the meaning of authenticity. Let's examine them.

The most familiar of these Japanese terms is *wabi sabi*, and it is complex. If you break the phrase up, we have our first clue. *Wabi* is a term that connotes loneliness, solitude. Think of living in nature, away from the frills of society. *Sabi* means ordinary, the very suchness of the everyday, and takes into account imperfection, the aging process that exemplifies the impermanence and fragility of life itself.

Put them together and they add up to the very soul of authenticity. In art, *wabi sabi* means finding beauty and meaning in nature, and even more specifically, in a rustic, unglamorized actuality, incorporating the imperfection and decay that is prevalent in nature and as important as the glory of a flower. Beauty is not seen as perfection, quite the contrary. It is the flawed nature of it that contributes to its value.

There is probably no concept more important in explaining the Zen of Art than *wabi sabi*. If the artist is a practitioner of this concept, he embraces the imperfections in his work that give it its flavor and zest. Recognizing this, the artist does not attempt to fix the crack, stain, or blotch that may have occurred as part of the process of making the work. He lets it be, as it is essential to the life of that work of art.

We have all experienced this when we say "something is so perfect that it does not look real." It looks artificial and inauthentic. In painting we know it is prudent to add a bit of black to our mixtures, transforming our palette from neon to muted, softer, off-bright colors. The more tonal the color, the more real it feels. Remember, the atmosphere on earth, which makes it possible for us to survive, is the ingredient that turns neon-bright, airless pigment into the muted, tonal notes we adore. They please us because of their authenticity.

In Zen philosophy there are a series of aesthetic preferences that are associated with *wabi sabi*, and they are interesting to think about. Before I enumerate them, though, I want to note that these preferences may be more illustrative of Japanese aesthetics than strictly promulgated by Zen philosophy. They are assumed to be Zen pronouncements when they may more accurately be described as cultural proclivities.

Japanese culture favors minimalism and tonality, and the Japanese aesthetic partiality is for subtle, understated, weathered, textured, and relatively tranquil imagery. When I say Zen style, you may imagine a tranquil living room with soft muted colors, simple furniture, an absence of clutter, and the lack of discordant notes; this would preclude disturbing or off-putting imagery. Another example of the Japanese aesthetic bent is the Zen garden, a minimalist, unadorned, textural space created with a linear pattern achieved by combing the earth enhanced with strategically placed rocks and other solid or shaped elements.

Though the Japanese favored style is associated with Zen theory, I do not believe it necessarily obviates more robust Western approaches, trends, and tastes. Though subdued and tonal treatments may be found in Western art, we find many other favored examples of decorative, patterned, colorful, and dramatic imagery. The latter may still be created in the spirit of Zen, though not emblematic of the Japanese preferences associated with it.

As I have expressed, Zen aesthetic principles can be extrapolated as an attitude that informs artistic practice but does not necessarily define the outcome. Above all, I treasure the *path* that Zen professes without limiting it to a specific artistic *destination*. There are many roads to truth, and truth looks different from varied points of view.

That being said, let's elaborate on those Japanese components of *wabi sabi*. We can define them as aesthetic criteria relevant to Japanese arts, and as attitudes and approaches, relevant generally.

***Fukinsei:* Asymmetry, irregularity.** This is an enthusiasm for recognizing the true nature of things and not trying to correct or perfect them. In art, this is achieved by being yourself and expressing yourself directly, without artifice. A conundrum: what about an artist who focuses on the geometric? Would using a ruler be a violation of Zen? I don't think it would bar it as an absolute, but the Zen principles might prefer a straight line made by hand with its inherent quirks.

***Kanso:* Simplicity, no clutter.** In art, as I have said, simplicity means staying true to your inspiration and not covering it up with extraneous notes. That doesn't mean one's work can't have a lot of detail, but the Zen aesthetic calls for baring the truth, not cloaking it.

***Koko:* Weathered.** The Zen aesthetic does not relish shine or luster, rather, the quality of a worn, lived skin. Many artists share this fondness, but some do not. Most painters, for instance, prefer a dry surface, not a glossy one, which appears glitzy or cheap. But there is a time and place for everything, and there is a time when a glossy surface may be just what an artist needs to express his truth.

***Shizen*: Natural.** Nature is such that we do not tire of admiring it. Not so with exaggerated or outlandish attitudes that may interest us for a time, but which we eventually turn away from. The Japanese proclivity is toward the natural, but that is not a prerequisite or imperative for art. For some artists, the fantastic unnatural is what they want to talk about. This predilection is overridden by *Datsuzoku* (see below).

***Yugen:* Subtlety, not obviousness.** The Japanese prefer subtle, understated imagery and art. There is definitely beauty in subtlety because it invites us to seek the meaning, which engages our intellect and senses. Some art wants to smack you in the face though, and that's okay.

***Seijaku:* Quiet, tranquility.** Here we have a way to categorize the Japanese aesthetic dismay for noise, a quality more sanguine to Western ears. Visually, noise is translated as clutter, excessive detail, perhaps riotous color. In Zen, it is the mind that yearns for quiet and tranquility, not the artwork. Can a quiet mind create a busy artwork? This sounds like a Zen koan. I will let you decide the answer.

***Datsuzoku:* Free, unconventional.** This aesthetic principle is the most important of all because it clarifies that though we may have aesthetic preferences, art is about truth, and truth can only be realized in a climate of openness and lack of bias. So, artists, realize that your truth trumps all rules. (See discussion about *datsuzoku* in Chapter 1.)

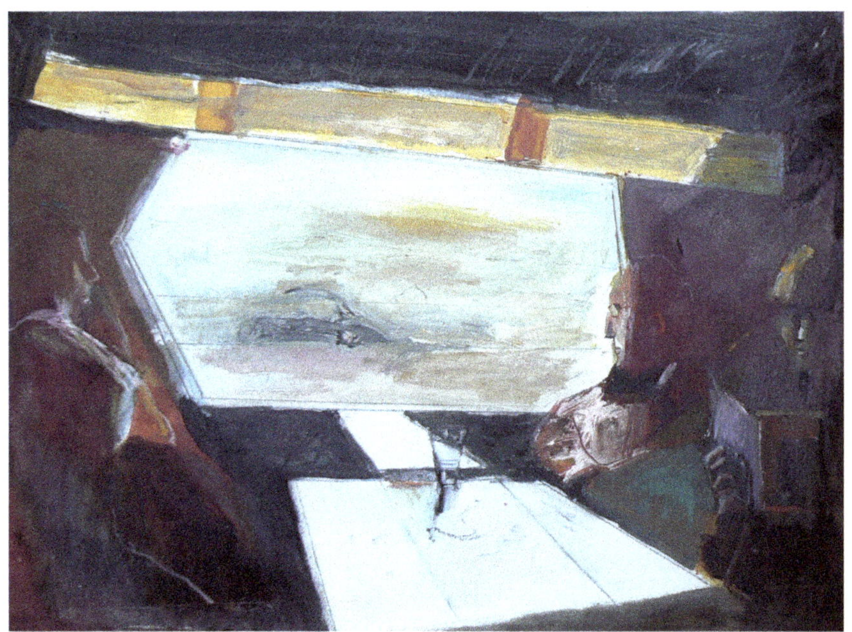

The Compartment, 2010, Pastel, 18 x 24 inches

When I was looking for an artwork that expressed authenticity in my body of work, I remembered a drawing that I sold many years ago to a woman who loved it. About a week after I delivered it, I heard she had suddenly died. The piece is called *The Compartment* and is a pastel of people on a train. It is very dark, but something about it seems true. I now see why she liked it so much. It is not prettified or enhanced, there are mistakes and unpainted sections, but it feels honest, a captured moment in imaginary time, a *wabi sabi* piece.

A note about painting—it is popular now to distress painted objects, to scrape and dull the paint so it has a more *authentic* feel. It is true that there is something very artificial about paint itself, a gooey material that can be harsh, overly oily or creamy, and just unctuous and distasteful. I encourage painters to experiment with a limited palette and to think about taking the neon out of their paint by adding white or black, whichever may be more appropriate, to achieve a more tonal *wabi sabi* quality. At times bright primaries may be just what is called for in a particular work. I am merely suggesting experimentation with softening and toning agents as well as approaches in addressing this concept of authenticity. These practices are not necessarily preferred, but they offer the artist another choice within a rich artistic vocabulary.

❧

In our modern culture, especially in the United States where commerce is probably at its highest concentration, the effort to sell things coincides with a definitive idea of what is valued and therefore marketable. We have extra thin models appearing in magazine advertisements, often presented in a most exaggerated manner, quite far from anything we would call authentic. Even though these models are selected for their unusual beauty, the images of them are often photoshopped to make them look even more unreal and certainly less like the rest of us ordinary mortals.

This represents a very different point of view, quite the opposite of the Japanese concept of *wabi sabi* that finds beauty most decidedly in old, weathered, distressed objects, and in the unadorned and natural. It is not surprising that elders are respected in Japan while they are shunted aside in America where attention is focused on the young and moneyed people who have the means to buy goods. This emphasis on commerce reflects a totally different value system and creates a wholly different culture and morality. It puts its mark on everything.

The consumerist philosophy filters into art and seeps into artists' studios where the desire to aggrandize, prettify, glorify, and embellish may fall like a vapor over the artist as she works, tempting her to falsify or overdo or overpolish the work. We are all influenced by the culture we live in, and unless we remove ourselves from its reach, we cannot help but be influenced by it.

Lately, museums, curators, and promoters, in their urge to make money for their institutions, are taking the work of artists and showing them in a manner that usurps the artist's vision and exploits the work to attract paying viewers. The work of Vincent van Gogh, who sold only one painting during his lifetime, is now being featured in so-called immersive displays that proffer entertainment at high ticket prices.

I recently read that the merchandising of the artist is reaching new heights with a museum collaborating with a perfumer to sell a scent using van Gogh's signature, taken from his artworks and made part of its brand. This approach is a pure and unadulterated desecration of the legacy of a magnificent artist who lived in poverty and struggled for the love of his art. It not only pollutes the artist's vision, it gives viewers a false sense of what art is really about. This is quite disturbing to me as an artist who struggles with issues of authenticity. How can the artist remain faithful to his work in the context of this greed? Do we have to bow to the commercial to be successful?

As an artist I can tell you that these influences are pernicious and hard to resist. The urge to prettify is strong and relentless; we want to make work that others will admire. To make something that is true, strong, and *un*pretty, yet deeply expressive, takes courage, wisdom, and self-respect. No one likes to be rejected, that is undeniable.

The nexus of art and money is a tricky one. Eons ago when artists painted images on cave walls, they had no notion of actual compensation, though they might have been inadvertently negotiating with the gods for favorable outcomes in the form of good rain or weak enemies. Much later, court painters were employees, making art for a fee and providing a much needed service before photography usurped them. Artists that followed them made art that was not commissioned and chose their own subject matter and treatment. But necessity required that they prove their talent by selling these works. And the need to sell them caused the dilemma that all artists face who want to make art as a career. Do you please the audience and get paid or please yourself and languish in poverty?

How can we be authentic given this conundrum?

When we choose "art for art's sake," make something that is true and we recognize it as such, as authentic, we are proud. We have gone against popular culture, bucked commercialism, and done something for love. It doesn't pay the bills, but it makes our days important. As Polonius said in Shakespeare's *Hamlet*, "To thine own self be true." The artist who does just that sits beside Shakespeare—and van Gogh—in heaven.

Grace

The Oxford English Dictionary defines grace as "benevolence towards humanity, bestowed freely and without regard to merit, and which manifests in the giving of blessings and granting of salvation." Let's unpack this. Grace is succor and aid that is granted to someone who does not necessarily merit that gift. If the gift was merited, it would be a recognition or an award. Because it is given, not earned, we consider it to be a blessing or perhaps a kind of unconditional love, a true gift, not payment at all, a privilege and an honor.

The concept of grace, the benefit of divine love, is associated with Christianity, not specifically with Zen, but there are parallels. Through Zen practice we may enter a state of grace, which ultimately is one of receptivity. As we open ourselves to the moment, regardless of whether we conjure an image of the divine or associate anything beyond ourselves as a benefactor, our openness brings us into a state of grace. In essence, being in the moment is consonant with being in a state of grace.

Life itself is a state of grace, and we need only be immersed in it to receive the message. As applied to artmaking and creativity, one might say that the kingdom of the divine is there for the taking, and all we must do is turn the radio on to receive the message. I have spoken about this in relation to inspiration, which is everywhere present. We must tune into it to catch it, and once we do, it falls on us like a glorious sun shower.

In *The Creative Path* I talked about how the artist prepares herself for her practice, noting that creativity is not a feature one turns on and off. You cannot tell when inspiration will come. Meditation and simple observation are tools the artist uses to sensitize his organism and make sure his antenna is always on standby. A seemingly unrelated and innocent phrase, look, or image may trigger the network of the emotional and physical nerve center in such a commending way that it becomes the genesis for the artist's next creative project.

These pings come often when you are not looking for them and rarely when you are, as self-consciousness has an abnegating effect. The more relaxed and otherwise occupied you are, or in other words, the more you are residing in the present moment, the more likely are they to call on your consciousness. Don't people often say that they get their best ideas in the shower, swimming pool, or while walking the dog? That is because these pleasurable activities have us safely tucked in the arms of the moment, and when we are relaxed, we are our most open.

I am delighted at how ideas come calling. People who view a certain work ask quizzically, "How in the world did you think of that?" My answer is that I didn't. Something occurred to me, and I followed the trail of crumbs the universe laid out for me. This is what Picasso meant when he said, "I do not search. I find."

Exactly right. You cannot find by searching. You must let your art find you. Would you call that grace? I would.

Where does an idea come from? Literally, anywhere. Anything you see can be a spark. It may be just a pretty or awful sight to someone else, but for you, in a moment, it hits a psychic nerve. The vision has a meaning to you alone. You connect it to something that is important to you.

This is not always something hefty and significant. It can also be playful and fun. Here's an example from my work. I used to like to go on eBay and look for odd vintage items that I could incorporate into my work. Since I was making small figurative sculpture at the time, I would key in the search words "doll parts" and look for items I could incorporate into my creations.

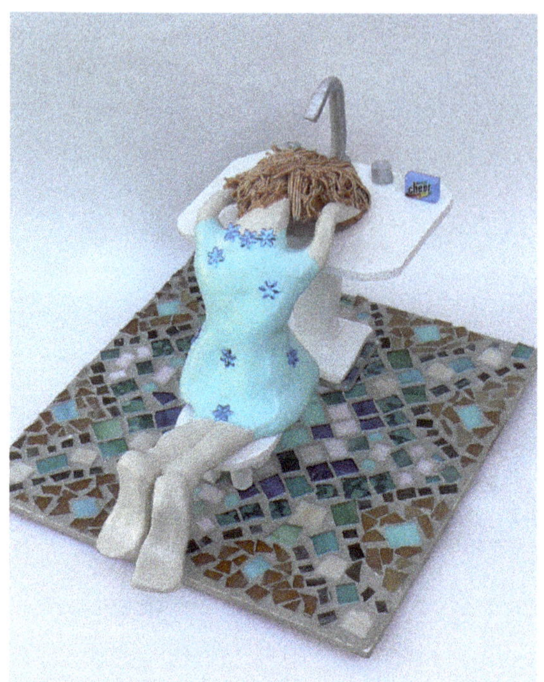

Cheer, 2005, Ceramic and glass, 6 x 12 x 12 inches

One day I stumbled on a little item for a doll house—a box of Cheer, which is a laundry detergent, a brand from the past. I immediately had the idea to make a little sculpture of a woman with her head in a sink, and to put that box on the sink. That she would be washing her head in cheer tickled my fancy, and I set about creating the sink and figure in clay.

Now, if I had the intention of making a work of art on the subject of a positive attitude, would I have come up with this same work? Probably not. I found the subject in that little box of Cheer and employed it to arrive at that meaning. The point is that you use what you have and follow the path as it presents itself. Sometimes the inspiration is an idea and the image follows, and sometimes the image is the inspiration and the idea comes later.

As a relevant aside, I mentioned that I sometimes seek vintage items to incorporate into my work. There is something to this. Vintage or historical remnants are emotion generators, and additionally, they have that *wabi sabi* quality of being worn or used, which is also aesthetically pleasing. To take something from the past and bring it into the present moment is a resonant act for an artist; we are giving it new life, new purpose. This is inspiring.

Artists often take old canvases, either their own discarded images or those created by another person, and paint over them. When I have done this, I always leave something of the prior image poking and peeking through to acknowledge and honor it. There is a term for this in the language of painting. It is called pentimento, a word derived from Italian meaning "repentance." Repentance is an act of "reviewing one's actions and feeling contrition or regret for something one has done or omitted to do."

The actions we take have consequence and significance. Recognizing this imbues our choices with purpose—even the one to use an old canvas. My cognizance that I am carrying over something from the past as I paint over what was elevates the importance of what I do to it. I am not merely covering it, I am taking what was to a new and better place.

Creativity penetrates every aspect of an artist's life. It is not a light switch we turn on when we enter the studio and then shut as we move on to other activities. That is because ideas come to us when we least expect them, when doing simple tasks like shopping, cleaning, exercising. All we really have to do is to turn our creativity light to *on* and just go about living.

Isn't it exciting to think that you can go hiking today, swimming tomorrow, or just take a nap, and your art will find you wherever you are? In fact, it might be lying there in wait on the trail or come to you in a dream. This makes the down times as potentially fertile as the hours you spend at the easel. The entire world is your studio. The secret of grace is that our ideas like to surprise us. When they do, we are wonderstruck and feel that we've been blessed. We are grateful, and there is no better soil for creative work than that. It is also, I might add, the best soil for growing a happy life. Gratitude is the sister to grace, and we will talk a lot about this as we continue.

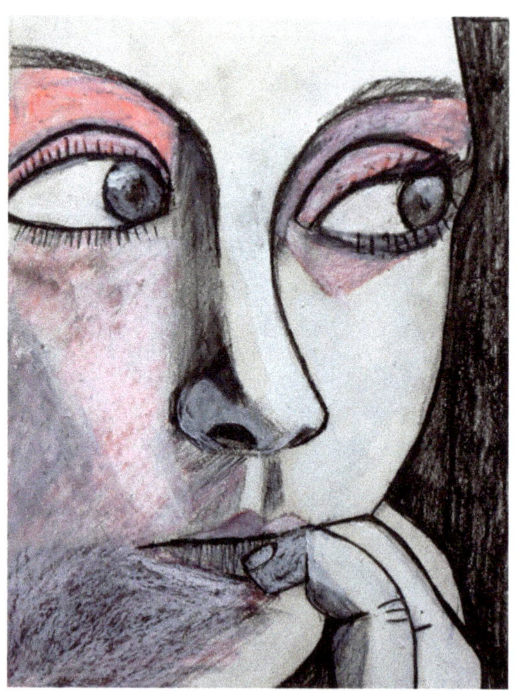

Seeker, Pencil and crayon on paper, 12 x 9 inches

THREE

Self

"I yam what I yam and dats all what I yam."
—Popeye the Sailor Man

Identity

Who am I? A question that plagues every human as we make our way, take our spin in the universe. Albert Einstein, who few would dispute was a very smart man, volunteered that "There are only two ways to live your life. One is as if nothing is a miracle. The other is as if everything is a miracle."

The fact that no two humans are genetically, physically, intellectually, or in personality and demeanor, alike, is pretty remarkable, and argues for Einstein's second choice. Not to mention that number two is surely the fun way to go. I go with miracle.

So how do we humans become acquainted with our miraculous individuality? Well, we are blessed with consciousness, which means that simultaneously with being ourselves, we can watch ourselves being. We can also shape our being, our behavior, and yes, even our consciousness.

I apologize for quoting Popeye and Einstein on the same

page, but Einstein wasn't necessarily better than Popeye at evaluating himself. Popeye was perhaps a bit more simplistic, as he was not an equivocator. He was who he was, and that's just okay. He might even have been a little bit Zen.

As an artist, your identity, at least your signature, is unmistakable. No matter how you endeavor to paint like x or y, what stares you in the face after a most valiant attempt, is, well, you. Your arm swings to a certain rhythm, utilizes a very specific pressure, and your eye takes you precisely where it wants to go. People who look at your work can recognize you instantaneously—the color mixtures, for sure, and especially your touch. Every artist touches the canvas in an entirely different way. You can tell by looking at your brushes, the bristles of which take on a peculiar sway, and at your palette, which stains a certain color depending on the percentage of the hues you unconsciously favor. Some very savvy observer could do an analysis of your tools, never look at the canvas, and tell you what's on it and who did it. Ha! The artist caught in the act.

We can't help ourselves. We have to be ourselves and that's that. In my book *The Creative Path*, I talked a bit about following an urgency my teacher called the wanting of your eye. That's not quite the same thing as the conscious you wanting something. It is much more than that. Your conscious mind is full of all kinds of dos and don'ts, not to mention a whole passel full of shoulds and musts—the ego, you know, telling you what will show you off to the world.

But the eye of the artist is the creative urge itself, propelling that hand to make those textures and select those colors. Those choices come from the whole organism, and some may be conscious, but not all. Familiar is more like it. Because of who we are, we tend to make similar choices, trod the same territory, so to speak. But this happens without our making it so. It just is.

And that's where the Zen part comes in. We can relax and let that eye want to its heart's content and not try to engineer it at all. We can call it "going with the flow," but we might also call it "being who you are" because, truthfully, it's the same thing.

I think this is why artists who paint people get told that every painting looks like the artist. It's just easier to recognize those similarities with figurative art. But if you look at the work of any artist in any genre—landscape, still life, abstraction—the very same is true. Even the pots and the trees resemble the artist; they look how the artist would look if he were a pot or a tree. This may sound silly, but it's not. Our egocentric brains see our reflection in every grain and molecule. We're obsessed.

Remember, we can only be ourselves. The art we make helps to define what that is, who we are, and why we are making pictures rather than drilling teeth or driving taxis. We see ourselves reflected on the canvas or hunk of wood or whatever medium is our pleasure.

Since our art is a projection of our inner life, it can teach us who we are, illustrate our inner life for us. Our art can tell us what matters, what we need, and what roads we are called to follow. Look at your art and read your soul.

People say that artists find themselves through their art. How exactly does this happen?

Imagine a group of artists in a studio painting the same still life from a collection of inanimate objects sitting on a table. How can you learn anything about yourself painting a pot? you ask. Well, it turns out that each artist, using the same set of objects as inspiration, approaches the task from his or her own point of view. Each finds what is important or interesting about the subject, but the choices are quite personal. One is fascinated with the light as it defines each object; the next sees a set of interlocking shapes; the third, a set of textures and patterns.

After many still lifes and portraits, landscapes, and abstract works, an artist begins to realize what matters to her, what she always seems to be going after. She may then set out to be more selective about her subject matter, choosing and changing it to accentuate and stimulate these tendencies and desires. This is the inquiry process the artist goes through in setting her intention.

I have discovered that I am decidedly risk adverse. I do not like roller coasters, skydiving, motorcycles, murder mysteries, horror movies, dark alleys, haunted houses, flocks of large birds, and other scary things. I don't mind bugs, am very fond of most animals, especially dogs, goats, deer. I find cows endearing too. I adore front porches with rocking chairs, lemon trees, any body of water, vistas, craggy mountain trails, folk music and opera, find musical instruments very beautiful, love the Northern Lights and transparency and translucency wherever they may appear. I am called to paint windows, doors, mirrors, reflections in bodies of water, and any other surface. I am entranced by innocence, and this makes me want to paint children. I love sunrises and sunsets, and this makes me want to imagine the day the universe was born and the day it will die. I like irregularity, but not excessive deviance. I could go on and on.

How does this translate into my artwork? Subject matter: women and children, imaginary places, idealized objects. Color: light-filled but with a touch of black to temper and soften. Texture: dry, tender, flat. Always seeking: the glow, simplicity, essence, gorgeousness, miracles, and magic.

Here's a typical piece that exemplifies my work—it's me, I guess. It is called *Astonished Girl*—"astonished" being a word that pertains to my life as an artist—astonished and wanting to astonish.

When I finished *Astonished Girl*, I recognized it immediately as mine. I was satisfied because it expressed my aesthetic so well—the simplicity of the line defining the dress, the hands drawn tenderly but not overdone, the blocks of color that define the contours of the face and chest, that look of bewilderment that has my name.

It pleased me. When we are able to project who we truly are, we are pleased.

I give you this example of my personal work and encourage you to analyze your own inclinations and how they are

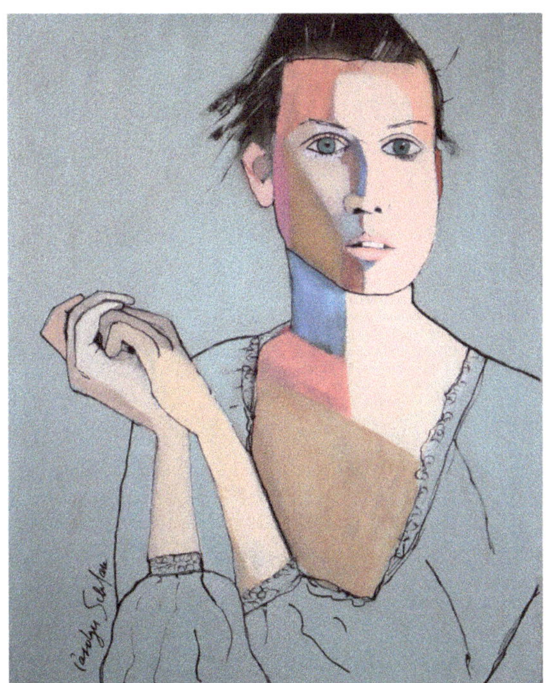

Astonished Girl, 2018, Oil on canvas, 30 x 24 inches

expressed in a similar fashion. We are each a complex package of so many things, and how they come together to create our art is just marvelous, wondrous, and helps us to appreciate both art and the artist in a much more meaningful way.

I think we can all agree that we want to know ourselves. We are self-conscious and always comparing ourselves to others. One of the ways to learn who you are is to take note of what you like. Your loves. Your obsessions. Being an artist makes that job very easy.

I am a big believer in journaling, list-making, note-taking, and the like. As artmaking reveals who you are, take note. Ask yourself:

What subjects interest you?
What shapes do you keep making?
What color paint are you always running out of?
What is difficult for you?
Are you dark or light?

What artists are you jealous of?
What would you like to create more than anything?
What's off your list?
What bores, frightens, tickles, astounds you?

As Popeye insinuated, you are what you are and are therefore limited, but recognizing it is the first step to making those limits magnificent. Do you magnificently, that's the ultimate win.

Here's my haiku about where art can take you:

Art is a secret
passageway,
a portal
to the cave
of your soul

Why do I picture the soul as a cave? I see it as a sanctuary that we guard from the sight of others, that we attempt to protect. I always imagine caves as containing art on their walls too. So, somehow, it makes sense.

As you develop as an artist, you are continually adding to what I like to think of as your treasure map. The spots on the map are all the jewels you discover along the way. And what are the jewels? They are the emblems of your individuality, and they are radiating with recognition as you discover them and make them your own. They are who you are, what you are made of, and what you have to leave the world.

Follow your art into self-awareness. Use it well. Read your own work and seek out the messages contained therein. Little by little, the clues will lead you to that special place that is you.

Ego

"Humility is not thinking less of yourself.
It's thinking of yourself less."
—C. S. Lewis

Ego is commonly thought to be the I, the self, sense of self, who you think you are. Ego is that part of the Freudian classification system that describes the psyche or personality. Along with the id and the superego, these three parts constitute the psychic makeup of the individual.

In this system the id is the province of the basic instincts and impulses and includes wants and desires, urges and bodily needs. The superego is on the opposite side of the spectrum, functioning as judge or conscience, and might govern ideals and spiritual goals, for instance. And the ego? Well, the ego is the moderator, the mediator between the baby (id) and the parent (superego). The ego is the referee, you might say, and keeps everything in the psyche copacetic. The ego is rationality.

Freud came up with this system to explain how the psyche operates, not to condemn or disparage any of these three elements. Yet ego is seen as a very derogatory term. Having ego generally refers to having an inflated sense of self, and egotism is the condition of being self-centered, primarily concerned with oneself over others.

The way ego is understood in Zen thinking differs somewhat from the way ego is defined by Freud. Zen views the ego as an obstacle to the creation of a more spiritually centered life. Ego is synonymous with one's sense of self and the excessive importance given to that individuation. Self-absorption is what prevents us from achieving compassion and furthers a sense of separation from others. The goal is to transcend ego, so as to come into harmony with the universal consciousness so we may live a less self-centered, more altruistic life.

How does this pertain to art? I have discussed how artists naturally develop a signature by virtue of their unique interests and vision. This is a function of their nature and is not to be discouraged or disparaged.

Ego can and often does play a destructive part in the development and growth of an artist, getting in the way of his spontaneity and keeping him from discovering formerly unknown aspects of his creative ability. We can get so "full of ourselves" that we stop being artists and become imitations of our former selves.

We can become associated with a particular style or subject until it no longer has any meaning outside ego identification. We can lose our spontaneity and become hacks. We can make the act of creativity as mundane as stamping out a product on an assembly line. Ego can rob us of what makes us artists in the first place—the calling to express, the drive to make our being manifest.

Ego can make us go dead, that's for sure. So how can we rid our art of ego and reawaken?

Zen talks of emptying the mind, but emptying it of what exactly? Presuppositions, judgment, habitual thought and action, secondary rewards and expectations like ego gratification. What is left when this emptying occurs? The moment. Scrubbed new, we sit in the experience of now, unencumbered by past experience or future expectation.

Suffice it to say, this is a difficult state to achieve, and the artist who achieves it will tell you he spent the afternoon creating in a dream. He looks up at the clock and wonders where the time has gone and how he managed to make this work in a flash, seemingly without effort. The word *anatta*, meaning "not self," is a description of this state of mind where the ego is unattached to the moment. Wonderful as this is to experience, it is a rare phenomenon.

I love to draw from a live model and have experienced this

state of empty mind many mornings when I sat with others drawing. Part of the impetus is the short amount of time we set for each pose, sometimes no more than a minute, so truthfully, there is no time to think. One must just take pencil in hand and act, make a fast line, and then another. There is no time to correct, certainly not to be neat, so the most one can hope for is a remnant, a snatching of what we see and feel in these brief moments.

The moments are feverish. We are rushing to express what we love about what we see. There is a directness to it that is exhilarating. And we don't expect to be terribly successful. How could we be in this abbreviated effort? Not having the expectation is another key to ego numbing. We're just having fun, doing our best, and seeing what happens.

This is less true for the longer poses, say the twenty-minute ones where much more can be accomplished. These drawings are often less compelling than the five-minute ones because they lack that feverish spontaneity. But the ego suppression is still in force because, really, can you create a masterpiece in twenty minutes? (You can, but I didn't tell you that.)

In the whirl of the studio with the clock racing and the time to make magic evaporating, I enter a seemingly egoless state of mind. My being is riveted on the paper, for therein lies the blessed opportunity to capture the beauty revealed in this moment of existence.

Ego plays such an enormous part in the life of an artist. Though all humans experience the judgment of others, not to mention self-evaluation, artists are held to a particularly high standard. Not only are we being evaluated, our work, which is expressive of who we are, is likewise under the microscope of critics, both professional and not.

It's a wonder we can take the chances necessary to create art. In fact, we get inured to the criticism to come, deciding that our desire to express ourselves trumps any fear of rejection.

The irony is that we must take chances in order to succeed, and this means pushing our egos out of the way so we can create. This is no small task.

The truth is that stepping aside and letting the work speak is the way we succeed; we make music by not tooting our own horns. This is the puzzle of artmaking, and it can be expressed in many ways. Here are a few of my mantras, phrases I have repeated and shared with students of painting, but you can extrapolate them to whatever medium you employ:

Learn everything you can, practice technique, repeat and refresh, then just throw it away when you step up to the easel. It will find its way onto the canvas without your help.

Instead of making the object, make the environment for the object to appear in.

Instead of painting what you see, paint your feelings about what you see.

Always go indirectly. You will reach your goal much faster.

The high road is the long road. Skip the shortcut.

Without ego, you can achieve your heart's content.

Don't try, just do.

Step aside.

Let go, and let ____ (you fill in the blank—God? Spirit? Soul? Ancestors?)

The Zen attitude is one of trusting that your identity is a fact—just like climate is a fact. It does not need to be asserted or proved. It just is and will express itself no matter whether you try to manifest it or not.

Meditation is preparation for this quieting of the ego, but you do not have to sit cross-legged and be still to meditate. You can walk or swim or draw in a meditative state. In transcendental meditation, we are given a mantra to repeat that focuses our attention. My mantra, and I assume all mantras, are two-syllable words that when repeated slowly mirror the beat of your heart . *Ta da, ta da, ta da . . .*

Meditation teaches us to focus on the breath and the heartbeat, which are part of the autonomic nervous system that regulates involuntary physiologic processes including heart rate, blood pressure, respiration, digestion, and sexual arousal. Meditation can be accomplished in many ways. I have found that a slow rock in my rocking chair, my movements in sync with the rate of my heart, is just as effective as repeating the mantra. I do the "meditation rock" nearly everyday, and I recommend you get yourself a rocking chair and try it. Sometimes I close my eyes, sometimes not; sometimes I sip water and rock, look at the sky and rock . . . no matter. It is a centering and restorative exercise.

If you are well, you do not need to employ knowledge, effort, or skill to perform the autonomic processes. They happen by themselves. Meditation, no matter how or where or when you accomplish it, reminds us that our life continues without our intervention. We are allowing our mind to align with that effortless state. Therein lies its great purpose and value.

Humility

You may have taken part in a yoga class in which the teacher and students repeat the word *namaste*, which means "I bow to the divinity in you." You may also associate the act of bowing with Buddhist practice. The act of bowing is a sign of respect and gratitude that we extend not only to living beings but to everything that supports us, even the cushion we sit on as we practice or the walls of our room that protect us from rain and wind.

We can become so enmeshed in our own ego, in our successes and excellent choices, that we become overconfident and closed to the good advice of others. The non-technical term for this is being "over your skis," thinking a bit too highly of your talent or expertise. Sometimes it takes something adverse to correct this feeling of superiority, the idea that you can go it alone because you know best.

Imagine someone all puffed up with this feeling walking into a room and slipping on a banana peel as they move haughtily to greet their hostess. Something similar happened to me as I egotistically challenged a friend who told me she slipped and fell, only to trip myself a moment later and land flat on my bottom, twisting my ankle in the process. *What a fool I am*, I instantly realized. *I am no better than the person I mocked.*

Sometimes we need to be set straight and discover that we are not "know-it-alls" after all. We'd be well served to listen to others and pay attention, get off our "high horses" and perhaps make that bow to the universe.

The good in this is that a dose of humility has the effect of resetting one's course, and often, an important lesson is learned. A few days after I fell and twisted my ankle, I went back to the pool for my regular swimming routine and, of course, I found that my hurt ankle would not permit such an undertaking. I was forced to modify my practice to suit these circumstances and was able to invent some new exercises to replace the old. Now my routine is better than ever, as I realized I had become ossified in my practice. Thank you humility! I am now having much more fun in the water.

Sometimes going wrong is the only way to discover a new route. Sometimes failing is the only way to break a habit. Sometimes ruining a work is the only way to create a new way to begin.

If you always see yourself as a student, you will be in the best position to grow, learn, and adapt. It helps to be grateful for reminders from the universe that we are overconfident; these corrective messages are crucial to our development.

Sometimes the reminders are harsh and painful. But remember, they could be worse. I could have broken my leg. Instead, I endured a few days of discomfort but was able to laugh at myself and find new swimming exercises to enjoy. I am grateful. I bow to the step that tripped me, my swollen ankle, and the swimming pool too.

The Voice Within

Freud divided the psyche into three components, but I'm going to introduce a fourth. Perhaps it is derived from one of the three, a part of one or more, or not. I call it *the voice*. Here's what I mean:

Creating a work of visual art involves making one decision, one choice after another. This is surely true for all the art forms. Do I pick up the cadmium red light or the cadmium deep? How much of it shall I use? Is the paint thick or thin? Do I say dearth or meagerness in this sentence? Is this musical section a crescendo? And so on. I could give examples from every art form and so can you. I will stick with visual art here, specifically painting.

I am painting the head of a girl with her finger in her mouth. Why am I painting it at all? The pose has a poignancy I wish to explore. I have decided to use just a few colors—large swatches of them. Half of the face is in shadow. I absolutely know, without equivocation, that the eye in this dark section must be yellow, a light lemon yellow. I know exactly how to mix it.

How do I know this? From the fourth part of my psyche—the voice, which is a knowingness in me that tells me I must make the eye yellow. It is not a calculated guess or a good try. I am absolutely convinced of its rightness. Where does it come from and what does it mean?

The voice is me, the artist. The part of me that wishes to speak on this canvas knows what I want to say. The voice is my spirit guide standing behind me as I work, telling me to do this and that. You might say it is my intellect, but it is more than that because I can make millions of intelligent choices and they may all work just as well.

Yes, they may work, but they won't be me. My voice is different from yours, and it makes choices that are just for me. If the voice is not my intellect, what is it? My best explanation is that it is my character, my shape, my being, my very soul in action—all rolled into one. It is my essential self.

Being an artist makes this voice very present because of the great need we have to express and the myriad choices

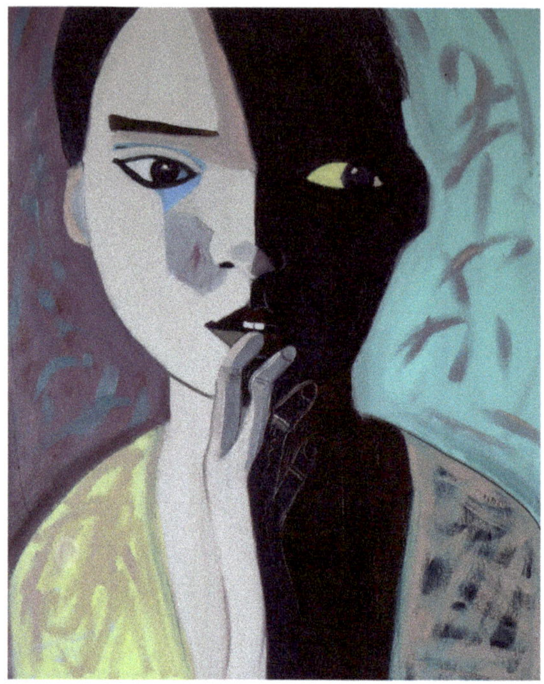

The Yellow Eye, 2020, Oil on canvas, 30 x 24 inches

presented by this activity. Also because this is one thing that is ours completely and totally. If we are making art for ourselves and not to fulfill a commission, we do not have to collaborate, equivocate, share, please others, be correct, or follow rules like we must do with so many other practices and daily activities.

As you create, I encourage you to recognize and honor this voice of your being that stands with you, leading you to make choices that are meaningful, beautiful, and worthy.

Freedom

Freedom is a very important concept to many people, certainly to Americans. We want to think we are free, and we celebrate that supposed freedom with flags and fireworks. But what exactly is freedom, and do we really have it?

I remember the lively discussion in philosophy class concerning free will versus determinism. The question: Do humans have any measure of free will or are their choices and outcomes influenced or determined by other factors? The behaviorists take the hard line, asserting that our behavior is greatly determined by influences, both external and internal. The softer approach gives individuals an element of choice while still acknowledging the great influence of all the determining factors.

Free as a bird, we say casually. But are birds free? Gifted with the sublime ability of flight, they still must take into account something "other"—their environment. Not to mention those silver tubes that share their skyways. If they are not free, can anyone be?

As artists, are we free? Presuming we are schooled in art, we have a whole compendium of information that comprises our "skyway." Dos and don'ts, rules of perspective and chiaroscuro, a collection of works by favorites and not so favorites that comprise our art file—so much stuff banging around up there. Then there are all the favorable and not so favorable reactions of our critics, art buddies, gallerists, publicists, agents, telling us they prefer this or that. It's a wonder we can decide to move our arm this way or that with all these voices barking out directions.

The good thing is that, for the most part, we are doing our art in our solitary space with no one watching. That does feel deliciously private and freeing. If I go right with the red, who's to notice or care? I don't have to hang the thing, do I? It's my secret.

The fact that an artist can work in this singular way is freeing. Much more difficult are occasions when you have to collaborate with someone who brings with them an entirely different set of rules and regulations. Almost impossible is when you are executing an assignment created by someone else or for a specific purpose.

Of course the artist can be that person orchestrating the show. He can be the player and also the conductor, a one-man band. He can be free, but only if there are no consequences, nothing at stake, no one barking orders or passing judgment. This is rarely the case, as even if all of these conditions are met save for the last, we are distracted. The last is the most difficult to achieve as often the artist is the one who passes judgment on his own work.

An artist is free when she is immersed, as much as possible, in the moment of creation. It doesn't matter what she did yesterday or will maybe do tomorrow. It doesn't matter that her last three tries were flops or that they exceeded expectations. It's a new day, and the Etch A Sketch has been wiped clean. In this new moment we are free to concoct a new vision. The more we can be reborn in the moment, the better chance we have for a great experience—but not necessarily a great result, as we don't yet know the obstacles we may face. But freedom absolutely grants us the best likelihood of a meaningful trip. (Note that I do not say enjoyable, as pleasure is not necessarily our intention. Meaningful, yes.)

Let's think on this cryptic quote by the Zen thinker Alan Watts: "Will and faith are two aspects of the same thing." And then this: "Life lives you, you do not live life. Everything that happens is of itself so." Let's break down this enigmatic quote.

The phrase "of itself so" has a particular meaning in Eastern philosophy. It is also referred to as *ziran* and translates as "naturally or spontaneously, i.e. without thought." This is the Zen way, and in a sense it makes the so-called dichotomy between free will and determinism an irrelevancy. We think we are shaping, making our lives, but are we? Watts thinks not. We perhaps are the characters in the play, but we have not written the script.

Maybe there is no script. Maybe there is no you. Or maybe the you is the script. In any case, there is no leader and no follower, no separation. Just life, of which you are part.

I looked up an Eastern concept I found in writings called choiceless awareness. A term discussed by Krishnamurti, this is described as a state of non-interference. Think of the organs of your body working in concert, each one fulfilling its specific purpose. You don't have to mind these organs—your liver, your lungs, your digestive system; all just do their jobs while you are pondering what to have for breakfast. What if you could allow other necessary processes to happen in the same way, automatically, without the intervention of conscious choice making.

Now let's apply this to artmaking. Is it possible to achieve this state of stepping out of your art's way, letting it create itself? Choiceless awareness is discussed in the literature as a possible byproduct of meditation practice, a state that might be reached by emptying the mind. To achieve it in art requires that the artist release himself from ideas of success and failure, from past mistakes and successes, and from any concern with the outcome. Then, and only then, can she access this highly creative state. My teacher recognized this (without knowing these specific terms or concepts) when he wrote the very last of his ten commandments of art: "Never worry how it looks." Without preconceived ideas or judgment, art is born free. How thrilling for the artist to get out of her own way and let art happen. The artist is the conduit, the channeler.

Ironically, you may imagine that the artist working in this way is without thought, driven perhaps by impulse or feeling. But I don't believe this is exactly the case. Just like the liver and lungs are working automatically, so must the brain as well, and thoughts will naturally occur as the artist undertakes his task.

In meditation practice, thoughts do naturally occur, as do feelings, but the practitioner lets them just come and go, gently continuing the meditation, maybe repeating the mantra. In the same way, the artist lets his art grow organically, returning to his inspiration, which is his mantra. The artwork comes into being without interruption or interference.

Kristnamurti asserted that choicelessness arises when perception is not sullied by ego. It is akin to that state of engaged perception, that "being in the zone" we discussed previously. In this state, the artwork is freely made. The artist is both maker and observer because he has partnered with nature in the creation.

This is a different way of looking at freedom. What makes us free is not our separation from that which is outside of us, not rebellion against the other, but just the opposite—our union with it. By releasing ourselves from ego (individuality) we become one with all, part of the fabric of the universe, and our work of art becomes another thread of creation.

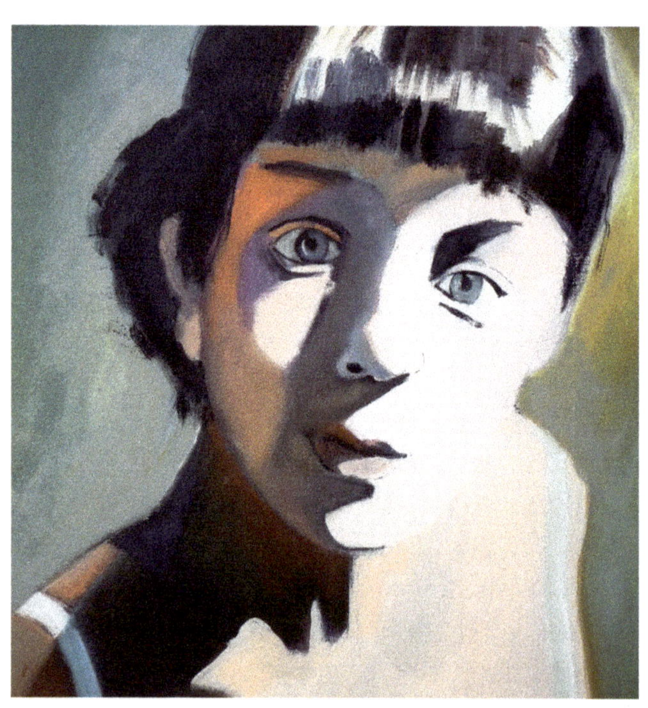

I Wonder, Oil on Canvas, 30 x 24 inches

FOUR
Practice

"Discipline is choosing between what you want now, and what you want most."

—Abraham Lincoln

Discipline

Discipline. I hate that word, don't you? It's such a hard, unpleasant word. Who wants to have discipline? No one, not really. We want to dance, play, have fun. Discipline is so stern, so punishing. It's an "eat your spinach" word, a word from a mean headmistress snarling at a beautiful young child. I hate to foist it on you, I really do, but, alas, I must. Maybe I can take some of the stigma away. I will try.

I started this chapter with Abraham Lincoln's wise words that express the idea very succinctly: Discipline is something you do today for an even greater reward tomorrow. Now this may seem to conflict with the Zen idea of being in the moment, but it doesn't.

Being in the moment is not a license to act frivolously. In fact, in the practice of Zen, sitting in meditation—what is called *zazen*—is decidedly a discipline and is highly recommended as a way to settle the mind and lead you to insights about your existence that will take you, hopefully . . . maybe, to enlightenment. Yoga teachers refer to their *asanas* as practice and to us as practitioners. We must continue to practice until we get it right. The question is: what's the *it?*

Ah. It. *It* can be many things. It can be perfecting your backstroke. Being a good friend. Learning to control your anger. Baking bread. Countless activities that require practice to . . . what? Learn. Do well. Shine. Excel. Amaze the world. Find peace. So many important and necessary goals.

So discipline—doing something you don't really feel like doing but think you should—is a "should" thing. I deal with this, as you probably do, every single day. I am a swimmer, and I use swimming as a way to keep healthy and also as a meditative practice. Remember, I mentioned earlier that meditation can take many forms. For me, I have to get wet. But so often I do not feel like it. I can feel myself resisting both going to the pool and getting into it. I have to remind myself again and again that it is important and necessary. Then when I get into it, I have to work against the resistance I feel to doing a full workout. Sometimes I give myself an excuse to do a shorter practice: *I worked hard yesterday, I didn't sleep well, I'll make it up tomorrow*—that kind of thing. But then I chastise myself and say, *Oh, Carolyn, just do it. You'll feel better if you do.*

Usually that works and I complete the workout, and yes, I feel better. Better because I did it anyway, and better because the swim really is healing, and my heart says thank you. I secretly maintain that I have tricked my cells into believing I am younger than I truly am. That's the extra piece of candy I give myself as a reward for a job well done.

Swimming, in comparison to other activities, is a rather easy discipline. Making art consistently is much, much more difficult; sometimes it feels like one has to move a mountain just to begin.

Take making a painting as an example. There's so much to it. Here's what the process entails: First, I have to have an intention, an idea for what I want to make, a starting point. Hopefully, I have received one of those glorious messages from the universe that I call inspiration. For the purpose of this example, let's say I have seen a beautiful scene while driving down the California coastline, a vision of a thousand blues, and that is my inspiration. Okay. Good. Next I have to figure out what size to make this piece. Is it vertical or horizontal? Will it be watery or dense? What foil will I use for the blues? Do I do an underpainting? Do I want it to be dry? Shall I use the linseed oil or not? And on and on. A million little decisions.

I have to stand at the easel, and my back hurts a little from the drive. But I'm determined. I lay out my paints and begin.

I can't just put down the blue, can I? No, I cannot. I know from many years of painting that I cannot go directly and quickly to my destination. I must take the long road, travel by indirection, and build to the blue so that by the time I get to it, the painting is begging for it. Only then will it sing like the thousand blues I imagined.

You may recognize or translate this concept into the more familiar phrase: "delayed gratification." All discipline is a variant of this; it's work one does as preparation for a future reward. And many of us find out too late that if we haven't put in the time and effort to prepare for a hoped-for result, it just cannot happen. We are actually shortchanging ourselves and obviating the possibility of such reward if we don't plant the seeds necessary to bring us to fulfillment. It's a process, you know.

So I work slowly, putting down different notes, trying them out. And I know instinctively that many are wrong and they have to go. It takes hours. I get hungry and tired. I have to stop and take a break.

I have to be patient. I have to be disciplined and keep at it. Maybe I work on this piece for five days. Maybe ten. Maybe I mess it up and have to scrape off all that good paint I put down and start again.

I won't stop until I am satisfied that I achieved a scintilla of what I set out to do. It may happen or it may not. If I succeed, I will give it a name and people will look at it. Maybe they will even admire it. But they will not know how much discipline and work it took to do it. Only I know that.

Remember this when you are inclined to comment or criticize the work of others. You don't know what it took for them to get there. You were watching a movie and relaxing while this artist was slaving away, trying to achieve that perfect blue. Be kind. It probably took a lot more gumption and discipline than you think to take the longer route, to go that extra mile. Not all of us do it, but we can all admire effort, discipline, and conviction. These are qualities that can lead to greatness. To IT!

Without discipline—dare I say it?—we are dilettantes, and we don't want to be that. Luckily, we don't want to be that more than we don't want to be disciplined. A dilettante is someone who plays at a task without real conviction, and that isn't anything to write home about. If someone called me a dilettante, I would hide my head in shame. Why do something if you're not going to put your heart into it and do it seriously?

That's what discipline is for—to help you put your heart and soul into everything you do. But it's complicated, and we need to peel back a few more layers.

Rules

Discipline is easy when you get to design the program, like I do with swimming and painting. When it's our choice, we can stop whenever we want to. But what if the discipline is ordained by someone else? A teacher, mentor, parent, authority figure—someone else laying down the rules for us to follow.

There's no avoiding this in life. As children we are unable to make all of our own choices. We simply don't know enough. Our parents are there to keep us safe and to steer us in what they think is the best direction. They are aided by aunts and uncles, teachers, mentors, religious figures, coaches, pundits, a long line of authority figures who are anxious to get in there and tell us what we can and cannot do. The rules, baby, the rules.

This is partly where our resistance to discipline is born. We don't want to follow the rules that someone else is foisting upon us. It makes us squirm, and before we know it, we're fighting the rules. Why? For just one reason: they are not ours. The rules may be sensible, even wise, but they are not ours. We feel victimized by them and want to rebel.

I am in such a situation as I write this. I live in a planned unit development that has some rules that date from ancient times, and they simply do not apply to the way we live today. They gall me.

I happen to have a neighbor who is a big believer in tradition and recently told me that I must obey an irrational practice because *it's the rule. So what?* I say to her. *Bad rules are made to be broken.* Suffice it to say, this does not endear my neighbor to me. She digs in even deeper, and we are at war.

But I do believe what I am saying. Sometimes we stick to rules just because we have always done so, even though they may have become irrelevant or no longer warranted. This may likewise be true for the rules we lay on our own behavior or practice; they may have become obsolete.

So, in light of this ideas, I hereby amend what I said about discipline. It's best to not forsake discipline or regular routines and habits, but to re-evaluate them in light of new circumstances. Just because you've always done something one way doesn't mean you need to continue doing it that way. If something that was advisable in the past has become a never-questioned rule, it may have outlived its usefulness.

It's a good idea, I think, to sometimes go wrong in questioning what you think is right. How else will you know if the aphorism is still true? Maybe it's time to turn it on its head.

An artist is a person who cannot, by their very nature, hew too closely to rules. They may work for awhile, but then it's better to chuck them. Otherwise, art would remain static, and new approaches, discoveries, and movements would never come about.

Artists have deep conviction . . . and then they don't. Think about the Impressionists. They discovered the exquisite potency of light. Even though artists had been walking in the light of day for centuries—judging from what was on their canvases—they failed to see it. Then one day, Claude Monet, nicknamed "the eye," became the eyes on the light of the world, and Impressionism was born. Many artists followed in his footsteps.

But one day some saucy artists who would later call themselves the Fauves—the wild ones—decided that the soft muted pastels that the Impressionists used to describe light was a rule that was no longer important. They took their bold, primary, nonpastel colors and plopped them down on the canvas, and Fauvism was the new hurrah.

Then, in due time, followers of the Fauves decided the colors were a wee bit too bright. Some even flip-flopped to the opposite extreme: a severely restricted palette and Minimalism.

Throughout history, we see episodes of utter conviction for one thing or another being exchanged for something completely different but with equal conviction. Classicism. Romanticism. Then Classicism Redux. That is the way of art movements, philosophical arguments, historical trends, you name it. Questioning and challenging the rules is the way to make change, and change is what leads to knowledge and wisdom.

You are thinking that I am negating what I had to say about discipline. Right? But let me convince you that I am not. It is good and important to have discipline and to work hard. I stand by that. But a caveat. Sometimes it is good and important to be undisciplined for the sake of experimentation, to check out whether your discipline is still useful and preferable. Perhaps your prior conviction has gone flat and something new and sparkling has appeared.

Be convicted in your discipline and be convicted in your rule breaking. Just don't hurt anyone. I like the late Congressman and civil rights activist John Lewis's call for what he named "good trouble": not conforming to bad rules, being open to change and to new wisdom, not settling, growing and asking others to grow too.

Don't overdo being a goody-goody. If you do your exercise diligently and regularly, it is okay to have a day of complete languor. Maybe it's even a good idea. After a solid seven days of swimming, even I give myself the luxury of a day off. I've earned it, but I remind myself that tomorrow, it's back to business.

And maybe if you, as a painter, regularly lead by indirection, letting your inspiration build and grow, one day just take the big brush and go directly for painterly exuberance. Who would I be to discourage you?

If you don't test your disciplines, your rules, they will become dogmatic and useless. They will no longer be convictions, only routine habits, and bad ones at that.

Yes, this is what I am telling you: order and familiarity are not absolutes. They can become dead ends. Work hard, be open, and bend with the wind. Discipline may make you competent, yes, but going beyond discipline to inspired practice will take you much further indeed. Maybe all the way to enlightenment. See my visual pun on the subject on the next page.

When speaking about concepts such as discipline, rules and enlightenment, it's best to do it with a light heart. What's more Zen than laughter, after all?

The Greatest Good

We love to rate things. The ten best this and that. We're always comparing and contrasting. That's how we figure things out. We

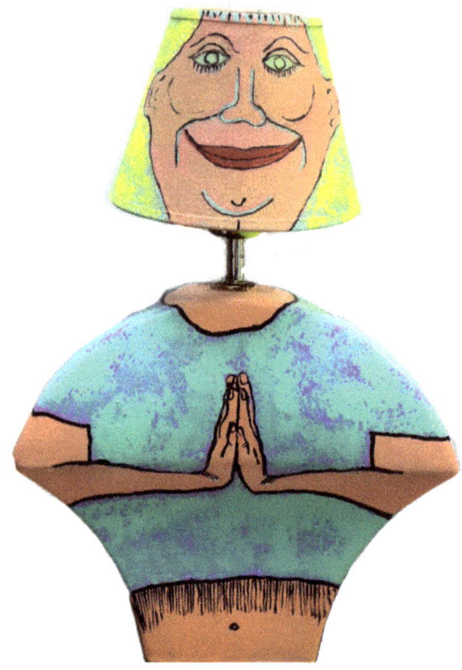

Enlightment, 2004, Painted lamp, 18 x 12 x 6 inches

need numbers, scales, measuring instruments of all kinds. We also love to give prizes and awards. Competition—it's endless.

Who do you love more? Aunt Sally or Uncle Bill?

Would you rather go out with Marilyn Monroe or Ava Gardner?

What food would you take to the island if you could only choose one?

Who's the best . . . artist . . . singer . . . writer . . . ?

And these are the easy questions.

Judgments are weightier than preferences. Our likes and dislikes change all the time and no one really makes much of it or cares. But judgments—that's another story altogether. They have import and influence.

Should the government provide for the less fortunate or should it be the responsibility of private industry?

Should people be free to choose or should society regulate the use of possibly dangerous things like guns?

Should wealth be shared?

Thinkers of all stripes—philosophers, politicians, scholars, scientists, sociologists, theologians, as well as just ordinary people—discuss these questions endlessly, but the questions are too difficult. There is no absolute right or wrong answer. They are all debatable, and different points of view can be justified and argued.

Some questions are unanswerable and will be forever debated:

Does God exist?

What is beauty?

What came first—the chicken or the egg?

In the course of our lives we have to make many decisions, and sometimes they are based on where we fall on the gamut of ideas—right or left or any point in between. Today we often get stuck on a certain side, a particular point of view or vantage point, and our thinking is prescripted and predetermined.

What criteria should we use to guide us? How can we be open-minded and free-thinking?

Some favor the utilitarian concept of the greater good. This concept is a numbers game—what is best is providing the greatest good for the greatest number. Sounds like an easy and noble prescription.

If the question were simple—should we save one person or five—the numerical standard would be automatic. But what if the question is: Should we kill one person to save five others? Think Hiroshima. If we use the greater good formula, the answer would be yes, but is that the most ethical formula? Making decisions based on numbers alone is not sufficient. It is clear that other factors must be taken into account.

Zen thinking values the community, but it simultaneously values the self. The greatest good would be something that is beneficial to both self and others to the greatest extent, and where no one is harmed. That may sometimes be an easy choice, but life poses much more complicated and questionable scenarios.

In art and in life, it is sometimes the case that you cannot please everyone or save everyone. We always want to exercise compassion, but choices must be made, and many of these are hard. Sometimes we must sacrifice something worthy for the greater good, and it is unavoidable. If we try to save everything, we may lose our way and wind up losing all.

In the following example, the greatest good theory may provide a guide:

Let's say I am making a painting of two figures—a man and a woman. My intention is to represent the relationship between them, and in this case my theme is regret. I paint the figures and the woman is beautiful. But there is something about the way I have expressed her that violates the theme of my work. You don't see regret. You see a beautiful woman.

So I have a choice: I can either change the theme and intention of my work, or I can repaint the female figure so she conforms to my original theme. Whichever way I go, I must take an action and make a sacrifice. But I am in love with my work; I don't want to change it. But my work isn't working; it's not delivering the message I intended, I remind myself. So I ask the painting: What is the greater good—that I remain true to my original theme or I morph you into something else? does this mean repaint the female figure?

Sometimes we need principles in our practice to guide us when facing hard choices, and this is where we turn to our discipline. In our art and in our lives, the more we step back and take a long look, the wiser will be our choices.

If I look only at this painting, I may choose the first option—remain true to my theme. But when I see it in the context of my entire body of my work, the sacrifice of changing the theme is less significant and makes sense. So too in life—taking the long look makes today's choice less crucial and monumental. We can make it up tomorrow. We can try again. It isn't the end of the world after all.

Perspective is what we're after. And this brings us full circle, back to where we started—daily practice. The routine quieting of our minds through any of the many forms of meditation is what enables us to escape the chattering of our monkey minds and settle into a peaceful contemplation that takes us to that long view way of thinking.

Things that perturb us today are like insect bites that we will totally forget tomorrow. Meditation helps us to rest in the big picture, take the long view, move from irritation to acceptance. Through practice, we can become peaceful and make choices that reflect our deeper truths and needs. Who knows, it may even deliver us to insight into the great unanswered but persistent questions.

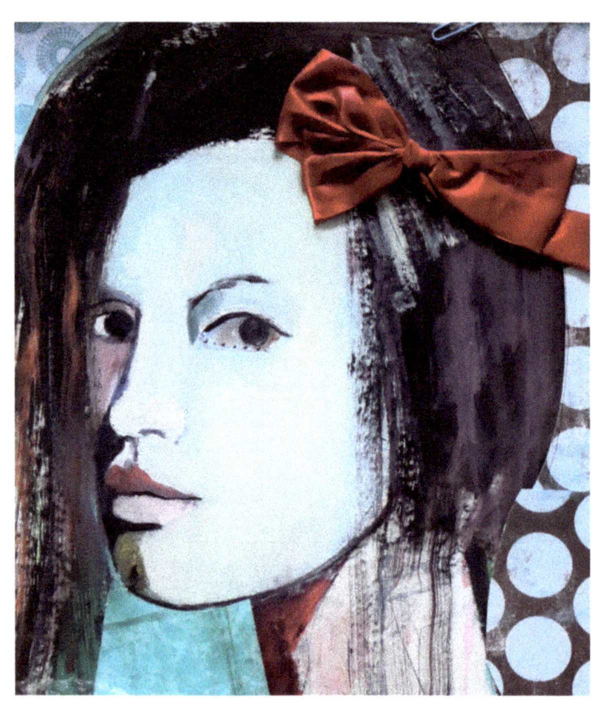

The Red Bow, Collage, 30 x 22 inches

FIVE

Courage

"I'm not afraid of death; I just don't want to be there when it happens."

—Woody Allen

I chuckled when I found this quote. It rang so true, a thought we might all have and never admit when we are trying to be smart and high-minded. But it's good to get down to the nitty-gritty, to the honest truth before we get too fancy.

We are all afraid. And what is our greatest fear? That we will die, of course. We will cease to be, and that is unfathomable, isn't it? How could it be that I—the consciousness that is thinking these thoughts, writing these words, doing all that I do—will disappear. I will miss out on so much, on everything. This is terrible.

But then I remember . . . there was a time before I was born. I know nothing about it and the world then knew nothing of me. I will just be going back to that time. I will not know that I am not. That is the consolation. The fear is in the knowing, the consciousness.

For all of our lives, at least up until we get sick, we take our mortality and stash it in a closet, probably at the back of the most inaccessible shelf. We can't be bothered with taking it down much. It's kind of like our box of mementos. We just know it's there, and we'll have to take it with us in case of emergency.

There are people who say they are not afraid of death,

though they do not welcome it. That's why we chuckle when we read that Woody Allen quote. These people are too busy living.

Ram Dass tells us in his wonderful book *Polishing the Mirror* that fear of death is anticipatory, part of living in the future. The only cure is to live in the present. He says that death is just the closing chapter in a book, the book of your life. You will probably spoil your experience if you try to skip to the end, won't you? But he also tells us—recommends really—to prepare ourselves to die consciously. The first instruction is to live fully and to "be present in your soul, not your ego."

That brings us to courage. My presumption is that it takes courage to live, and so we all possess it. To walk into the unknown, well, that takes gumption. Does it take more courage to be fearful and still press on than to proceed calmly through your days? Yes, I think so. When you plant yourself totally in the moment, let the past live in that box in the closet and the future be just a figment of your imagination, not of immediate concern; when you can just be here now, be comfortably ensconced in just this very moment—that seems doable and strangely to take much less courage. Isn't it actually much easier to be doing what you are doing and not thinking of anything else? Relaxing into the moment. You realize how much stress is connected to anxiety about the future. Why, then, is this so difficult for us?

A friend wrote to say that he had been reading one of my books and thinks I am brave. He obviously was telling me that he thought it took courage to write the book. Does it take courage to express yourself, to do creative work?

I'm pretty sure he is connecting courage with book writing because he is thinking of what I might face as a result of writing the book. Bad reviews. Lack of interest. No sales. The consequences. But when I was writing it, I was not thinking of what might happen. I was just trying to express my thoughts in the most cogent manner I could. Yes, I wanted to write well, and I guess part of this wanting to do well was connected to the book being well received. Of course I would prefer that to it being panned.

So ego is involved. Did it take courage to forge ahead? I guess you could say that I wrote the book in spite of the possible negative outcome, and that required some courage. But while I was working on it, I focused on the daily work and not on how my work would be received. If I had, I might have been too worried to take action.

Focusing on the future, anticipating a result, is clearly an impediment. Though I did not succeed in shutting down my ego, I looked past it so I could complete the task. Think of this not as not a "letting go" but as a "setting aside," which serves the same purpose.

When we are alone in our contemplation, thinking and planning our art-to-be, we are in the comfort zone, snuggled in our imagination. But stepping into the studio to actually make our vision concrete, now we are climbing out on that beam. I am thinking of that famous photo of construction workers sitting on a beam of a skyscraper they are building, their legs dangling in the air. (I hope you know it. If not, look it up and you will see what I mean. It gives me vertigo to think about it.) The situation is so precarious, and you can't help but imagine that any minute someone will fall. That's kind of how I feel when I leave my comfort zone and get to work in the studio. The task seems daunting. Am I up to it? It seemed so possible when I was thinking about it.

What am I afraid of? That I will fall? Change one letter. Fail.

We need to set aside ego to have the courage to express ourselves. I believe the courage can be found in the joy of the work, our desire to communicate something, and to communicate well. Not focusing on the future ironically gives us the best chance for a positive future result. We are getting out of our own way.

If we are able to do this—stay in the present even if the outcome is not as we might hope—we will still have the memory of the experience. I also believe that the energy of staying in the present is invariably reflected in the work we produce—another great factor speaking to the likelihood of future success.

So, when you get to the door of the party, you might pause a moment and take a breath, but don't stand there too long. Just step on in. It might be a blast; it might be a bore, but what the hell. It takes courage to put one foot in front of the other. But what choice do we have? All the goodies are behind that door.

It occurred to me recently as I was preparing work for an exhibition that being an artist is messy. No matter how much you try to stay clean and above the fray, it's a dirty business. Paint drips. It goes everywhere. You get excited, and it gets on you, in your hair, on your clothes.

Yes, artmaking is physically messy, but it's also emotionally messy. There's no way to stay in a pristine condition. You can't make art and not get messy. You've got to get in there and mix it up; otherwise it *ain't gonna* happen. No way.

And know this too: You won't want to put a mess out for the world to see. So making the mess is only the first step. Once the work is done, you're going to have to clean it up. You're going to go all out to make something wonderful, disregarding how challenging and damn aggravating and disruptive it is, in order that in the future someone will hang that work of art on the wall and be amazed at how lovely it truly is.

Not being willing to get dirty is the way to have a neat but lackluster experience. You've saved yourself the trouble, but so what? If you have courage, you make the godawful mess, and when it comes together and you look at it, you know it was worth it. How great does it feel to get clean and organized after all that hullabaloo you've created. It feels sensational. You're proud. You did it!

Courage—what is it and how do I get some? First, remember that the word is derived from the word heart—*coeur* in French, *corazon* in Spanish, *cuore* in Italian, *coracao* in Portuguese. Remember that and open the door with your heart, your love of art, your love of life.

Soldiers march into battle for love of country. Heroes jump

into frigid waters for love of their fellow mammal. Forgetting or setting aside our fear of failure, even death, for the sake of something greater, finer, worth giving all for—that's heart.

Years ago I had an exhibition in an airport, and I entitled the show *Have a Heart*. My mascot was a doll. I sewed 839 hearts on her. After the show was installed, I sat down in the airport at a nearby bench and watched a thousand people walk by in an hour and look at her and all the other pieces I had made for the show. I still remember the joy I felt thinking that I had just witnessed so many people enjoying what I had made—my imaginings come to life.

I felt so blessed. I had been so worried that they would think little of me and my work, make fun or maybe even laugh at me. But people seemed to enjoy looking at my little concoctions, and I even sold some of the pieces to passengers.

Basically, it comes down to this: If you don't take a chance, you won't know. You'll never be sure that what you do is worth anything, can move anyone. You'll just be in your head, left to your imaginings, and you will be wrong. If you do try to get out there, you will be surprised and joyful—that I guarantee.

Now let's continue. In Zen writing you will come across certain words that repeat again and again. Acceptance. Non-Attachment. Surrender. They are all related to this idea of courage and we'll take them one by one.

Acceptance

Let's assume you have the initial courage to put yourself out there, to express yourself in word or picture or any other medium. You want to express well and create something you are proud of. I think this is a given and would apply to anyone, regardless of their spiritual bent.

Do your best. Is there anything about that concept that might violate Zen principles? I can't think of anything because doing your best takes into account your limitations, which would include lack of ability, training, knowledge, etc. Zen encourages us to be in the now and to accept ourselves where we find ourselves.

What is acceptance? Is it admitting what is and agreeing to it? Does that mean we don't do anything about it?

I looked into this concept and found the Sanskrit terms for suffering and for its opposite—happiness. The word for suffering, stress, unease, dissatisfaction is *duhkha* and the word for pleasure, comfort, happiness is *sukha*. Here is the derivation of these terms: *du*=bad, *su*=good. What is *kha*? *Kha* is the word for the hole in the middle of a wheel into which the axle fits. If the fit is *su*, the ride is smooth. If it is ill-fitting, *du*, the ride is bumpy.

These words fit into our discussion of acceptance. Will life offer us a smooth or bumpy ride? Of course if we have a choice, we all will choose the smooth ride—the pleasantries, joys of life. But we realize that this is not always possible. *Duhkha* is prevalent, even foundational to existence. Very often in life, the axle does not fit, and we cannot fix it. We should certainly try, but short of our success, what do we do?

The Zen way is not to resist what is, but to accept. We may use our intelligence to change our circumstances, but just fighting them by denying them is useless. Accepting what is, in fact, gives us the best chance to change because acceptance is not resignation—it is realization.

Let's say I've been working for a while and everything has been going beautifully. I am in the *wu wei*, and I am happy. Then I become aware that I've got something here (ego alert), and before I know what has happened, my happy trip has been forestalled. I've messed up, the drawing or painting is moribund, and I am lost. Something is not right. I keep trying to fix what's wrong, but this piecemeal approach doesn't work. I try and try, fiddle and putter, but it isn't working. Why not?

The likely reason is that my mindset has changed, and I have veered onto an alternate road. I have elements in the work that I like, but others are discordant. The piece does not hold together. Since I am attached to some of what I have wrought (my ego approving), I am not really willing to change it. I am holding on to what I have. I am stuck, immobilized.

What to do? Finally, with courage—or maybe just plain frustration—I get the big brush and whoosh—I annihilate my bad trip. I am back in the soup, the abstract, that beautiful beginning we talked about, and I can take a breath and continue. This action is liberating. I am now free to do better than before. I am no longer fixing. I am creating.

This has happened to me myriad times in my creative career. At times I have strayed so far away from my inspiration, gotten lost, and yes, had to have the courage to return to the beginning to get back on track. To keep true to your art, you have to be true and honest. You have to accept that you have strayed or gone wrong, and you have to stop resisting and simply do what is necessary to continue. This is the meaning of acceptance, and it is not a negative; it is a life-affirming, inspiration-affirming prerogative.

Here's an example of transformation. I once painted a doll-like figure with yellow shoes. I loved the yellow shoes, but the rest of the painting did not work. What to do? I took the big brush and whoosh—I struck out all but the yellow shoes. Then I built an entirely new image around them. I took the happiness of the yellow shoes and let them infuse all the other aspects of this new work.

Think of acceptance in this way: acceptance is a predicate for moving forward. Sounds wrong, doesn't it? If you accept something, you tend to think you are stuck with it. Well, not exactly. It just marks the present. It is where you are now, in this moment. You have this level of skill, understanding, commitment. Not forever, just now.

By placing the marker, accepting the now, you are liberated

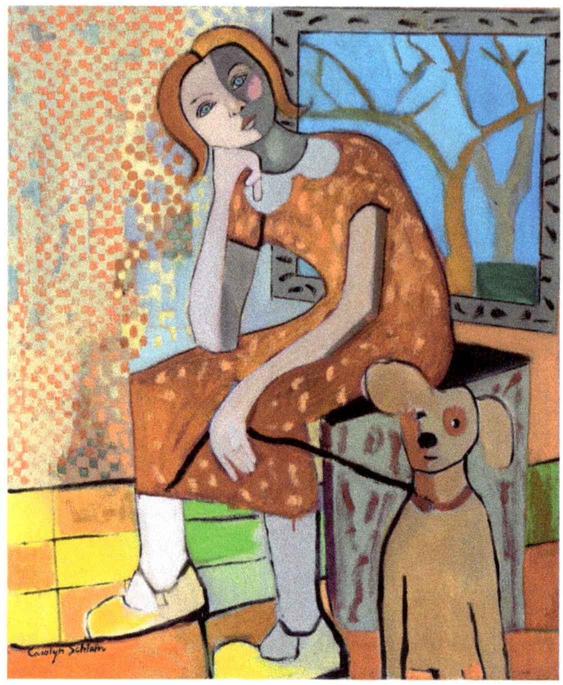

Girl with Dog, 2016, Oil on canvas, 46 x 36 inches

to move forward. Learn more, try something new, expand your repertoire, your horizons. Why not?

Denial is what keeps us stuck. Acceptance is a clearing, a statement of truth, and it sets you free to roam anew. It is a cousin of our next Zen concept, nonattachment, which we turn to now.

Nonattachment

If I command you to not think of an elephant, what comes immediately to mind? An elephant, of course. You may not have been thinking about it before I gave the command, but now you can think of nothing else. In fact, I have commanded you in the negative to affirmatively think about an elephant. So, likewise, can someone be told not to attach? Whatever does this mean?

Most humans form alliances, relationships, friendships, love affairs, and have desires galore on a daily basis. No one is suggesting that we stop doing things that are integral to our happiness and development. The problem is not with the attachments; it is with the expectations we form about them. Expectations belong to the future, and as we will discuss in our chapter on time, the future is but a mirage. Forming expectations about what will happen is the dangerous part of attachment. Why is that? Because our attachment is not to the thing itself but to a future version, result, or outcome, and this keeps us from enjoying the only real version—the one we are now experiencing. Expectations may even adversely affect how something ultimately turns out, if it turns out at all.

This sentiment comes to us in many formats, print certainly, as many authors extol living in the present. But it also comes to us in song. Apropos, I found this song in my Broadway piano book from the musical *La Cage Aux Folles* by Jerry Herman. The title is "The Best of Times." Herman assures us in the first line that the best of times is now. I encourage you to look up the lyrics and sing out. (Zen messages may be found anywhere, even on Broadway.)

As Herman reminds us, it's much more advantageous to not get attached to a particular dream of some deep-sought reality lest it not come about or something occurs in the nearer future to interfere. Best to just let it, as another music-maker, John Lennon, reminded us, . . . be.

The best laid plans . . . you know the rest. Something always happens to throw us a curve. Nothing turns out exactly how we imagine it will, does it? It's always a little different. Well, it has to be different because every moment we enter a different dimension, and everything looks different.

I am so aware of this when I am making art because I so much want my piece to turn out exactly as I have hoped it will. But no, the red I thought would work in the upper corner is too dark and too warm. It seemed like a good idea, but now that I see it, no, it's not right. I try orange. Better, but too bright. A browner orange might be better, and YES, it is, but the light is coming from the right. I add white. Now I'm getting somewhere.

The painting commands me to follow its route. I started it all, and I had a destination in mind, but now I see that I need to forsake it. I need to listen and follow the painting's commands.

When do we make our greatest discoveries? Oddly, not when all seems to be progressing well. No, not then. Often, at the lowest point, when all seems lost, and I just chuck it all and try something new.

Nonattachment. Can you see how it can lead to something new? Something that is unexpected? When you have no expectations, well, anything can happen. The universe says, "I bet Carolyn will really love this," and then it gives me an idea, a word, a phrase, a color, a shape that I never ever could have summoned.

In artmaking, giving up our attachments is often easier when we do not assign that much importance to the work to begin with. That's why we often prefer the pieces we dash off. They are done quickly, and we toil less. In the end, looking back, we may prefer them to the grand works we labored over and had lofty expectations for.

You will likewise feel this way about events in your life. The things you wanted the most often don't work out as you'd hoped, while things you cared less about turn into your very best memories. This tells you to ease up on your expectations, assumptions, prescriptions, all of that, and just do your thing.

The word "surprise" is not a Zen word, but it is one of my favorites. Like most people, adults and especially children, I adore a surprise. What do you feel when someone says, "I have a surprise for you"? Of course, it could be good or bad, but we pretty much assume it is good. If it was a bad surprise, we would use a different word. We'd say, *Sit down, I have some bad news.* But for a surprise, there's no need to sit. The most common response is to jump up and down with glee and say, "What is it? Do tell."

We love a surprise because it is not expected; it's a gift. It could be anything, and that's exciting. It very much could be something new that we don't already have. We're hoping we're going to love it. Maybe it's a puppy.

In art we have something that resembles a surprise. Some call it an accident—a happy accident. We are doing what we usually do, plowing those well-trodden fields of ours, when something goes awry. Maybe I've put the blue on my palette where I usually put the red. Without looking, I fill my brush, and wow, I never would have thought blue, but it looks sensational. Surprise!

Sometimes the happy accident happens because you didn't have what you needed. *I'd like to paint today, but I have no white, so maybe I'll just staple some fabric fragments onto the canvas. Wow, that's amazing. I love it! I'm going to do that again tomorrow, even after I get the white paint.*

I gave an example in my book *The Joy of Art* of an artist who had such an epiphany. He went out for a walk between paint sessions and discovered upon his return that his maid, in the course of cleaning the studio, had set down a recently completed canvas on its side instead of right side up. He was astounded. Unexpectedly, the artist was able to see his canvas in an entirely new way, and it set him on a totally new course with his work. The artist was Wassily Kandinsky, who was instrumental in creating a new art movement.

Surprises. Accidents. They are happenings that detach us from our habits. And that makes us better and takes us into new realms. Think of it as a surprise party. You thought you were going for dinner, but surprise, everyone who loves you has shown up for you. That's what making art can be and also, when you think about it, what a good life feels like.

Imperfection

Imperfect. Doesn't that word imply that there is something that could be considered perfect? Without fault? Flawless? The dictionary recognizes this as an impossibility when it defines "perfect" as "having the required or desired elements, qualities, or characteristics, as good as it is possible to be." So perfect isn't perfect, is it? Is it just almost perfect?

If nothing is altogether perfect, how can something be imperfect? Isn't everything imperfect if nothing is completely perfect?

Should I end this discussion now? No, this is just the beginning. If there is no such thing as perfection, why the hell are we striving for it? Maybe we are just striving to be less imperfect? Does that make any sense?

We need to do some redefining because an awful lot of us go out everyday and strive to be perfect—look perfect, act perfect, make perfect art. Don't we?

I heard about a stained-glass artist who always put a deliberate flaw in his stained-glass windows to remind himself that nothing is ever perfect. When you think about it, telling everyone about the purpose of the deliberate flaw meant that he did think his windows were perfect. Otherwise, they wouldn't need a deliberate flaw, would they? That was kind of egotistical, if you think about it.

I am of the opinion—though I may be mistaken—that the Jewish custom of having the husband smash a glass at the end of a wedding ceremony serves to remind us, on this happiest of all occasions, that there is suffering in the world. We know that there is suffering, though we continue to dream of perfect worlds, perfect art, perfect relationships, perfect brides and grooms, and myriad other perfect things, even perfect mundane things like a perfect lunch.

Let's try to name some good words to replace the word "perfect." How about "good"? A good lunch. Is that good enough? Not really. It's just good, not perfect.

How about "great"? Great is better than good surely, but is it perfect? Well, not quite.

"Near perfect"? That's redundant if perfect isn't really 100 percent perfect.

How about "extraordinary"? Then imperfect would be what, just ordinary? Nope.

Everyone kind of agrees that nothing is perfect, but do they believe it? We all need a more attainable achievement we can strive for then. Perfection just doesn't work.

Do you have a suggestion?

If nothing is or can be perfect, that's a relief. Let's chuck that concept totally.

Frankly, I like the word "best." That makes sense to me. I can't be perfect, but I can be the best me. I can make the best lunch available. I can paint the best painting of today.

Best is conditional. It's not absolute like perfect is. Best is only for now, and better may be here tomorrow.

Buddhism exhorts us to be our best, to follow the path to enlightenment, to be kind, thoughtful, compassionate, moral beings. It is rooted in what we can be, what we can achieve, not impossible standards we can never achieve.

I always think of making art as an honorable profession. We are so lucky as artists to be able to freely express ourselves in this remarkable way. So we really owe it to the universe to do our best always, not settle for easy solutions, and endeavor to exceed ourselves. In this way, we honor the gift we give to the world. We honor our viewers by giving them the best we can muster. We honor ourselves when we endeavor to not only "do *dharma*"—do what is right and just—but to do the best we can. Living this way and making art this way brings us the ultimate reward, and if there were such a thing as perfection, it would be this: being the best we are able to be in every moment we are given to make art, eat lunch, or just feel our breath.

One more thing, though, about being best. People—and artists—are often under the mistaken perception that if only they do more, they will arrive at perfection. *If only I keep going, I will get there* is the lie I comfort myself with. But it isn't true. Sometimes going on will set everything back, will ruin the good we have already achieved. Best does not mean more. Sometimes it means less and often it means stop. We can only go as far as our imagination and ability will take us in this moment.

I like artwork that is unfinished. Unfinished means that the act of creation is still happening. Perhaps it has now passed to the viewer. Work that is over-finished often seems dead, lifeless. Trying to make it perfect just killed it.

The whole idea of finishing is a myth. Nothing is ever finished. We could go on redoing the same painting *ad infinitum*. But we don't. We have to stop sometime or the paint would be a mile thick. So why not stop when the work is as fresh and new as a spring morning. Unfinished, but lovely.

The baby is in the womb about forty weeks, and then it is done. More time would not make it better. So too, the work on your canvas or in the wood shop tells you when it is ready to be born. You start to get the labor pains and are forced to take a step back. *Oh no*, you say, *but I am not finished*. The thing is—the artwork is, even if you're not. You'll have to get pregnant again. You remind yourself: *Nothing is perfect*.

Before we close on this subject of perfection, I will tell you a little anecdote. A friend who was visiting me recently remarked that she had passed by a neighbor's house and noticed he had put out the most gorgeous flowers. I knew the house she was referring to as the occupants are always improving upon their prior flower displays with one even more glorious. The next day I passed by the house on a walk with a neighbor, and I related my friend's remark about how stunningly perfect those flowers were. She laughed. "Look a little closer," she said, "they're fake." Indeed, those perfect specimens were actually flower-shaped lights.

The actual flowers were, of course, imperfect, but you might say they were perfect in their imperfectness. Nature gives us a spectacularly varied array of plants and flowers, and it is in the vastness and individuality of the collective display that we find perfection—a perfect earth, with every flower playing its imperfect part in the harmony.

This is a cautionary note to the visual artist. Trying to make something look too perfect has the effect of making it seem artificial. Reality has bumps and cuts and marks and is rarely perfectly symmetrical. Even pairs of things, like eyes and breasts, have slight differences. When we try to correct nature, we do it an injustice, and this deadens our work. When we celebrate the quirks, the anomalies, the individuality of each blade of grass, we are celebrating life itself. We are celebrating ourselves.

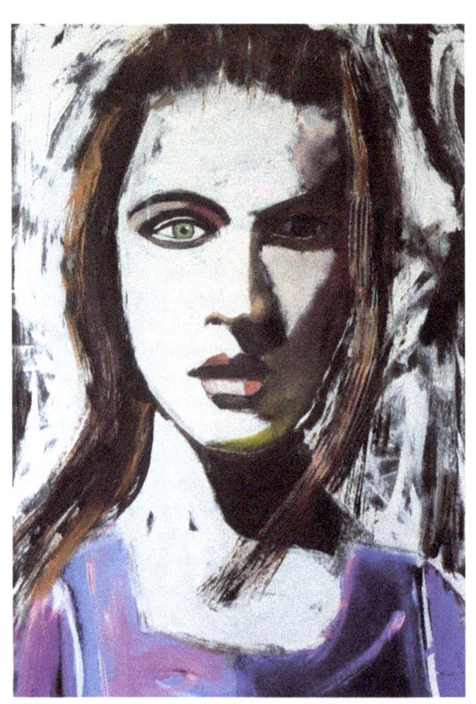

Struck, Oil and house paint on board, 32 x 20 inches

SIX
Change

"There is a crack in everything. That's how the light gets in."
—Leonard Cohen

The quote "No man ever steps in the same river twice, for it's not the same river and he's not the same man" is attributed to a Greek philosopher, Heraclitis, born in 544 BCE. Realizing that everything and everyone is in a constant state of flux is pretty remarkable for a thinker of his time, before modern evidence of evolution and the space/time continuum was ever conceived.

Let's now zoom forward to the nineteenth century and counter this epigram with this famous one by critic and writer Jean Baptise Alphonse Karr: *Plus ca change, plus c'est la meme*, or in English, "The more things change, the more they stay the same."

What are we to believe?

If we forgo absolutist thinking, both statements can be supported. Yes, certainly, change is constant, as every moment is slipping away as we try to capture it. Yet, also, some things seem to remain and are, if not constant, then persistent. I think whether you come down on one side or the other depends on your concept of time. Take the long view and you see forces and patterns persisting over time. On the other hand, we can barely hold on to something—a thought or an event—before it morphs into something else, another fragile moment zipping by. We want to stop time, take ourselves out of the continuum of time so we can rest.

We are the river itself, flowing through our lives. We cannot stop the flow. That's why, I think, we like photographs so much, and visual art. The photo or work of art has done what we cannot do—it has captured the moment. This is so startling when you see a portrait by Franz Hals with a subject caught frozen in laughter for all time. It seems so odd and is the reason so few portraits show an animated face. To show animation stopped is bizarre—a game of statues.

Other art forms mirror the flow. You can play the same sonata many times over—stepping in the same river, so to speak—but at least it is a moving river. Likewise for theater and fiction. In visual art, the process to create the work is hidden, and we see only the last act—the frozen, still image. We love that we can return to a work of art and experience it anew. Because we have changed, however, we may see it differently each time, though it remains the same.

Examining the process of making art has engaged my interest for many years, and I have very much wanted to reveal to people how that process evolves. I have taken time-lapsed photographs of works to attempt to illustrate the zig-zag evolution of a work from beginning to consummation. I say zig-zag because it is never a straight line, and the artist goes forward and back until resolution is accomplished, and time, for that artwork, at least, has stopped.

Indeed, you would have to take an incalculable number of photos to truly demonstrate all the changes a work of art goes through. For the artist, making her work of art is like watching a movie. She is always simultaneously both maker and observer. One step clearly and irrevocably leads to the next. The first marks are foundational; they establish the placement of elements and the compositional imperatives, along with the basics—size, color, direction, and the like. As the artist continues, it is clear that all the rest of the ensuing marks, splotches, areas of color, etc. are refinements of these original marks. All the determinants are there right from the beginning.

As the artist begins what is to become a figurative work,

the marks are general and vague. As she continues to define the visual space, the image becomes more and more specific. We always begin every work of art with the most general and abstract elements and the artist then chooses how far to bring the specificity.

Knowing when to stop or call it quits and mark the piece done and ready for either the dust bins or the repositories of history is entirely dependent on the degree to which the artist desires to bring the work to a point of exactitude or what we call verisimilitude—in other words, looking as demonstrably a likeness of the subject as is humanly possible. There are artists who strive for photographic likeness to the nth degree and others who have no interest whatsoever in achieving an imitative effect. In fact, they would call it anathema, as they believe the purpose of art is interpretation, not imitation.

This disagreement is specious. In fact, regardless of the degree of accuracy the artist strives for, every work of art is a translation, at the very least, and most probably an interpretation. We are not gods and goddesses, and all of us make illusions. There is nothing real about the images we conjure. We just are skilled at making the viewer think so.

The most relevant point in this chapter on change is that artmaking (and lifemaking too) is a process, an evolutionary process, where one thing leads to another, continuing until it reaches a point of resolution or until we decide to stop. Nothing is truly ever done; conclusions are markers, artificial closure points, pauses. Then we are off to the next painting, which is really a continuation of the one that went before. Since we never quite get to the absolute with our work, it always lacks something and we always think we can do better next time; finishing one work is just the predicate to try again.

Since the stream of artmaking can literally go on endlessly, we have to decide, as artists, when our vision has reached its stopping point. Remember the Marcel Proust story of the writer who keeps rewriting his first paragraph and never advancing? It takes energy to advance our work as well as to know when a work has reached its maturation point and any additional effort will no longer be fruitful.

One day someone may look at all of the artworks we have created and see them as a continuum. They may analyze how we have changed and hopefully grown in our execution, how our vision has morphed, our concerns have shifted, our color has grown richer or more somber, our treatment more serious or frivolous.

While we are alive, we stand inside the circus ring and cannot see the whole show. We are in it, creating it, so those critics of the future may draw conclusions about us. Our job, as artists, as people who are alive, is to stand in the rain and get soaked, dance in the moonlight, sprinkle the stardust on our canvases.

We leave it to others to evaluate who we have been. We're too busy being it to bother. Leave the dream analysis to the shrinks. Your job is to make the dreams.

Failure

Living is hard. Being an artist is hard too. The Buddhists know this very well and assert very clearly that we are victims of delusions that cause us great stress, what they call ***dukkha***, translated as "suffering." Of course, humans suffer actual physical pain and all sorts of anguish caused by circumstance, accident, malfeasance, all the terrible things that can potentially occur in the span of a human life.

But when the Buddhists speak of suffering, it is not simply these emergencies and exigencies that cause physical and psychic pain. Even moments of happiness can become sources of anguish to us as we realize that they are fleeting, that change is constant, and that nothing lasts. We strive to possess things. We form attachments with other people, and then what happens? The people die; the possessions are lost. In fact, we do not, cannot ever possess anything. We are all renters, living on borrowed time, and everything is in a constant state of change.

This is distressing to us all, and the Buddhists offer us a way not only to understand this reality but to accept it and find a path out of this trap they call *samsara*—the cycle of birth and death.

Buddhism is based on what are called the Four Noble Truths. Here is a summary:

One

Life is impermanent,
and this leads to stress and suffering.

Two

The cause of stress and suffering is our desire, our attempt to resist the fact of life's impermanence. This state of suffering is called *samudaya*. We try to deny it, but this causes us to suffer more.

Three

The way out of our suffering is called *nirodha*: letting go of our attachments and illusions, and accepting change.

Four

The way to freedom from suffering and toward enlightenment is called the Eightfold Path. If practiced, it can lead to fulfillment and *nirvana*, "enlightenment."

Buddhists tell us that the path to enlightenment is comprised of an attitude and way of being that lead away from suffering and toward *nirvana*. The way includes three main components:

One

The Path of Wisdom

With insight into the state of our existence and acceptance, we choose to make the commitment to change our attitude toward life. (Right Understanding and Intention)

Two
The Path of Ethical Conduct
In support of this change in our beliefs, we conduct ourselves ethically. This includes the nature of our speech, the way we treat others, and how we earn a living.
(Right Speech, Action, and Livelihood)

Three
Mental Discipline
We endeavor to exercise discipline to achieve our goal.
(Right Effort, Mindfulness, and Concentration).

It's important to understand the use of the word "right" in this context. This is not "right" expressed in legal entitlements, such as the right to free speech. Neither is it half of the common dichotomy known as right and wrong. "Right" in this context is like the righting of a ship on the waters, a state of peaceful equilibrium that allows the boat to remain upright and progressing. So too, the human remains upright and progressing by coming to the understanding that life is change, that nothing is permanent, that time is an illusion, and that all we have is now. In the now, we are called to accept what is and conduct ourselves in such a way that we happily coexist with nature, including with other creatures and our fellow humans; we are called to act with compassion, to meditate, and to use other mental strategies to follow the path to enlightenment.

By doing all of these things, we alleviate our suffering, which is caused by our refusal to accept change. Instead, by accepting it, we have the opportunity to experience true fulfillment of our purpose, and in doing so, to come to bliss.

Let us consider what relevance this may have in the making of art. To extrapolate, I would say that mental discipline is essential to creative practice. To continually seek inspiration and knowledge from the world around us is an ongoing pursuit of the artist, especially pertinent in the development of a body of work. Identifying and clarifying what is important to you in your art, what you are striving for, what inspires and moves you—all of these processes are ongoing. Applying the focus and discipline to continually invigorate and better your skills, treatment, and imagination is a hallmark of artistic development.

What about the idea of ethical conduct? Does that have a relevance in art? I think it does. I think striving to be your best self, to stretch your horizons, to challenge assumptions, and to avoid superficiality, sentimentality, and excess for its own sake—all might be considered within the realm of aesthetically ethical artmaking.

Just as ethical conduct is driven by recognition of the path to enlightenment, aesthetically ethical artmaking is driven by the goal of authenticity in art—the desire to tell one's personal truth in the most expressive manner possible. Recognizing what art is would be the equivalent of the Path of Wisdom for the artist.

As we "right" ourselves, we are increasingly equipped to create the best art we are capable of. This does not reduce our daring in any way. It enables us to be free because we are focused on that purpose—our intention to express magnificently. In order to do so, we must know ourselves, be mindful, concentrate, and focus so our art may soar.

Failure in life is caused by the inability to accept change, which consequently results in undue suffering. Failure in art is caused by the refusal to accept what our work can teach us about who we are and what we want to say to the world. Always returning to the source and asking the question WHAT DO I WANT TO SAY HERE? is the key to remaining true to your intention. That is the pathway to success, which we examine in our next section.

Success

What is success? One dictionary entry says "the accomplishment of an aim or objective." That's way too vague for our purposes. The aim could be dastardly and the accomplishment deadly. No, that will not help. Here's another: "the attainment of wealth, favor, or eminence." Certainly, many people will agree that any or all of these constitute success. But again, not relevant here in our discussion of art and Zen.

Would anyone say that van Gogh was successful because his work sold for vast sums after he was dead even though he sold only one painting for a meager sum while alive? I daresay no one would attribute his success to that! What then? He was a wonderful artist and made works of art that are personal, imaginative, beautiful, expressive, unusual, and powerful. His accomplishment was the quality of his work that many now admire. Sadly, though he is now thought by many to be one of the greatest artists who ever lived, his success was perhaps never experienced or acknowledged by the man himself.

In fact, financial reward alone or even the awarding of favor or eminence will not assure any artist that he is truly a success. Only if she has managed to create as marvelous a work of art as she intended or hoped for would success be achieved. Money or fame alone would be insufficient. Likewise, it would be unfathomable to say that a spiritual person, say a Zen monk, would have achieved success by gaining any outward reward. Success would have to be thought of as the pursuit of a spiritual path and the realization of its rewards.

My experience has been that some of my greatest successes occurred when I least expected them to, when I managed to surprise myself and do something I did not intend or could not even have imagined. The more humble the intention, the greater the possibility of success.

I think we can safely assert that success is achieved when a goal has been accomplished. Whether the goal must be an important one is up for discussion. I won't dispute that growing a lovely rose can be a success if it fulfills a gardener's intention. We have many successes in life such as these.

Our focus here is on something more significant, more noteworthy. A successful life, perhaps. Or success with one's occupation. What makes one's life's work a success? That's what we are talking about. Does achieving happiness do it? Having a family? Finding love? Enjoying nature? Traveling? Making colleagues and good friends? All of these, no doubt, contribute to the assignation of life as a good one, and I think we can all agree that only the individual can determine what success looks like because it depends on what he is trying to accomplish in the first place. The loftier our goals, the less success we may acknowledge.

The prerequisite for determining success is intention. Without a purpose in life, how can one even qualify one's experience as a success? We might say that just having a purpose and attempting to fulfill it—in other words, being on a pathway to success—is itself victory. We may not reach an ultimate goal, but trying to get there, setting the intention, and following through to effectuate it makes success a possibility. We might say that the journey, in and of itself, regardless of the outcome, is all that matters and all that we can be sure of. Secondary rewards like money and the esteem of others may be valued, but they are indeed secondary.

The Eightfold Path put forward by the Buddhists requires the follower to make a significant investment in his nature and experience. Striving to be mindful, ethical, compassionate—these efforts in and of themselves lead to a successful life. They reward us in daily practice with feelings of love, respect, admiration, and caring. Just attempting them is a salve to negative feelings, sorrow, fear, loneliness, and heartache. Just following this path, as the Buddha suggested, is its own reward.

Now we ask: For the artist, what constitutes a successful career? Popularity? Skill? Innovation? The answer is the same: setting the intention is key. When the artist hews to her intention, she follows her own path to fulfillment. Success cannot be bestowed by others. No praise from others will convince the artist of her success when she knows she has not taken her work to the mountaintop of her expressive capability.

Change is constant and ever present. When we recognize this and accept it without resisting, when we craft an intention that will be our path and then follow it faithfully, success is karma. It is inevitable because we are in the flow of life and our art. We are not begging for miracles. We take what comes gracefully, and the smiles on our faces reflect the smiles within.

Think of it this way. Success is not a far off goal. It is inherent in the daily work we do to further our intention, to grow in wisdom and skill, to be honest, compassionate, and brave. It is not a distant dream or a future fantasy. It is already achieved in the doing and being that is our present.

Growth

Our lifespan seems very short, especially as we look back. So swiftly have we moved from childhood to adulthood and then into old age. How did it happen so quickly? If we look back with a smile on our faces and warmth in our hearts, we'll see that it is because we've experienced much, and we have grown, not only up but in and out, grown in wisdom and understanding, and we've made relations with others that have sustained us.

I recently got a telephone call from a woman I met at an artists' workshop twelve years ago. The workshop was only for a week, and during that time we were busy day and night working on our art. How much time did I actually spend with this person? I have not seen or spoken to her since the workshop. She called me because she was on my contacts list and I had recently sent out a video of an interview I did. She called to congratulate me on the interview and "catch up." We spoke for an hour and ten minutes, and we covered a lot of territory. It felt like we had just spoken at the workshop yesterday.

Where did those twelve years go? So much happened to both of us, yet we were able to pick up where we left off. In fact, she remarked that when she saw me in the interview, she thought I had not changed a whit. It's like we just zoomed into today, seemingly teleported. Apparently, we had made quite an impression on one another if we could be so friendly after a twelve-year hiatus. We have a lot in common, and we have followed a similar path. We are both artists.

Having talked to this lovely person, it brings me to a recollection. Who I was then? Who did this person meet? I couldn't have been that different because she instantly recognized me on the interview as the same person. A lot has happened yet I seem the same. I must be, but with one caveat—I have grown.

I look older, for sure. I am more confidant—that she remarked on. I have done a lot of art in these twelve years, written four books, many articles, done a lot of living. I have had myriad conversations, swum a lot of laps in the pool, read a bunch of books, and done a lot of thinking. Who am I? What has all this living done to me? It has made me more . . . more of the same, with some new shoots. What do they say in advertising? New and improved. I am a new and improved version of myself.

The tiny plant that was me as a child is now a tree with roots that go deep into the soil, maybe so much so that they have torn up some sidewalks. In other words, I have branched out. I am bigger, stronger, and my limbs now reach into the sky. People even far away who have never met me have seen my art and read my words. And in the spring, new ideas adorn me, like new leaves. Birds set down on my top branches to have a rest in my presence and to share a moment. Maybe even a flower appears as I create something that touches someone's heart. My tree has taken its place in the world.

I love to look at trees because each one, in my opinion, has a distinct personality. Some are frail and wispy, indecisive. Others are majestic and lofty. There is hardly an adjective you can think of that you cannot attribute to a tree. I recently lived in a community that has many beautiful and varied trees. There was one in particular that I related to, and I would chance by on one of our daily dog walks. I called it "perfect tree" because it is so symmetrical and balanced—a truly superb specimen. (Of course it is not perfect, just very special). I had such affection for it that I would say, "Good morning, perfect tree, you're looking especially lovely today." I would visit it as a friend, truly. I should go over and pay it a visit soon.

In order to grow strong and lovely, a few things are required. First, you have to plant the seed. Then you need good growing conditions—sunlight, good soil, all that. What does that mean in the human context? It means that if you want to grow in wisdom, strength, and confidence, you must plant these seeds early in life. Then you need to nourish them with air to breathe, good nutrition, and care—lots of light and lots of love. You need to nurture your ideas, your wishes, and your dreams to make them grow into objects of beauty, just like my perfect tree that does no harm whatsoever, standing tall and providing shade through all conditions, standing tall so a woman and a dog can pass by and say hello. This is not ego. Not indulgence.

This care you give to your soul is also a gift to the world. It makes you grow and also advances the course of civilization. Remember that. I am happy I have grown. Thinking of our lives in this way feels so good and so right. So poignant. I am touched that this friend from the past visited my tree today and I hers. She seems the same too, but of course I am not familiar with all of the myriad ways she has grown. We do not get to know that about too many of the people in our lives.

What does it mean to grow as an artist? We've tried a lot of things in our practices. Some have worked, others not so much.

Some have surprised us. Some early successes now do not impress. Others that we considered failures now look better; we misjudged them. We've learned a lot. How to apply paint, how to make it sing. Other things too. How to make a mess. How to go completely off track. How to revive a dead image. How not to. We've learned the difference in quality and experience between working from deep inspiration or just phoning it in. We've learned what discovery feels like. What pride feels like. What exhaustion feels like. We've learned to recognize in our work who we are, what matters to us, and most especially, why we are on this earth. I've learned what I, and only I, can create; you have too. In other words, we've uncovered our identity in our work.

We've also failed and learned how to discover why we failed, and then go on to do something utterly amazing. We've learned that failure is the best teacher of all.

To grow as an artist, we must not only create, we must read the lessons in our work. What are they trying to tell us? All of the codes are embedded therein. To decipher them, we have to look at all of it, check out what we were trying to say, what obsessed us, what we did again and again. And then ask, why? What was in it for us? Where did it come from? What were the messages we were trying to convey? They may be disguised, hiding out. We don't see them directly, but they are there. We must search for them like they are positions on a treasure map, and follow them to that cave I spoke about—the cave of your soul.

It behooves me to follow my own advice and look for the clues in my own work and show them to you. While we are talking about growth, I need to talk about progression. Though we continue to grow, this does not mean that we are always improving. Let's talk about one's earlier self. One can look back into the past and find examples of our best selves in action. As artists it is important to keep and revisit our early work because often, the best and purest examples of who we are were made before we became conscious of what we were doing.

Even though we grow, it does not mean that we will continue to do better and better work. We have more experience and can understand more, but all that knowledge can be an impediment to free expression; we can often get in our own way. In our youth, when we knew less and were less conscious, the channels of our emotions were less clogged with plaque and, as a result, we did amazing work. Value it all; it is all you.

I painted a lovely nude when I was a young art student. I saved it for many years because I found it tender, And then one day, decades later, I got the bright idea that I might improve it. I know that as you are reading this, you are absolutely sure of what I am about to tell you. Yes, you are so correct. I ruined it. What did I do wrong? I tried to define it. It did not need defining. I saved parts of it and repainted other parts. It was whole. I made it fragmented. In other words, I violated my own principles and stepped out of the creativity of the moment, out of the innocence and surprise of it to an entirely different occupation—no longer artist, now plastic surgeon. You've heard the phrase: "to second guess." It means "to judge with hindsight." What is hindsight? An understanding of something after it has occurred. That's what I did. I traveled back in time with a different mindset, and I destroyed the moment I created in the first instance. Definitely a mistake. What's the lesson here? As your Mom or Dad probably told you many times: "Just leave well enough alone." I will remember that the next time I get an urge to "fix" something. The better path is to create something new, even if the intention and subject remain the same. Just whatever you do, don't overwrite. Use a fresh piece of paper. Imagine it as a fresh day because that's what it is. Okay?

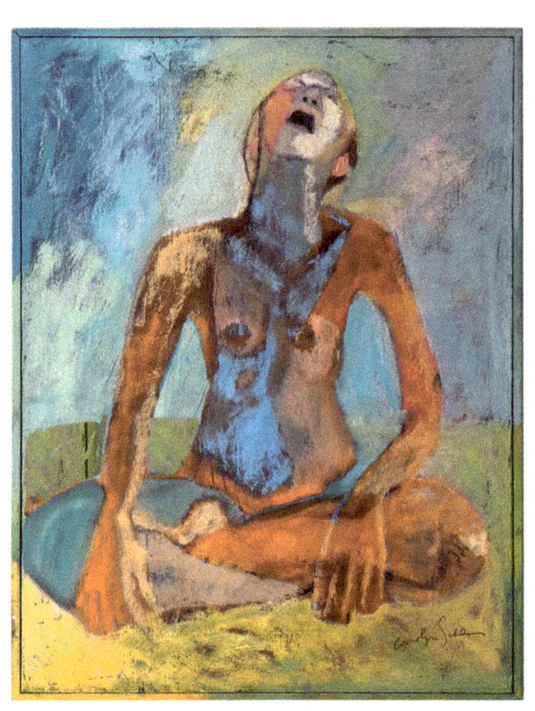

Buddha Girl, 2014, Oil on canvas, 40 x 30 inches

SEVEN

Joy

"Before enlightenment, chop wood, carry water.
After enlightenment, chop wood, carry water."

Here is an image I made several years ago of a woman sitting in meditation—*Buddha Girl*. The coloration is strange, and frankly, I don't recall what possessed me to use this preponderance of blue and orange, more suitable for a football jersey than a Buddha-esque figure. I don't have the painting anymore, having given it to a friend who liked it a lot more than I did at the time.

When I was looking for appropriate art for this volume, I remembered this work. I have often found that the work I dismiss as just average or humdrum in the moment resonates with me the most years later. Our point of view changes, and this is a good reason not to discard works that fail to please. I am guilty of having destroyed many works that seemed inadequate or perhaps had some fatal flaw—at least I thought so at the time.

This is surely ego, as I do not want what I consider inferior pieces to continue to exist as this somehow sullies the body of work that presents who I am. But I am happy that I did not destroy the woman sitting in meditation and that my friend saw some value in it and saved it from the dumpster.

From the point of view I am accessing today, I see this piece with more respect. Though the color palette seems weird, what

I do like is the expressive quality of this work. Have I said how amazing I still find it to look at a depiction of a human in paint, especially in idiotic colors like these, and find in it some humanity? After all, what is it? It is just paint molecules on a board.

Yes, if you break it down, that's all it is. But no, those molecules were hand selected by a human who had a point of view that day that guided her human hand to the right and to the left. And presto, out came this orange and blue girl with her head pointing to the sky.

You may like this piece or not, but do you agree with me that we cannot discern whether this orange-blue being is in agony or in ecstasy? Which is it? Is she crying out in intense pain or in orgasmic joy? Does she bemoan her life or exalt in all that befalls her? Which is it?

And this takes us to the larger question, which is: What is joy and what is its source and importance? How and why does it come to us? Surely, if it does, we are in a state of grace.

When I was very young, before art school sculpted my thinking, I made a drawing of a young girl flying through space. Feeling the exuberance of youth and the vast vista of possibilities at my disposal, this was my chosen subject.

What was the picture of joy to me as a young painter? Leaving the earth and flying through the sky, unattached to anyone and just feeling pure exhilaration. This is surely one version of joy—freeing oneself from suffering of any kind, be it from interference, disorder, or malfeasance. Flying free. Unburdened to the max.

We do seem to like that feeling we get from Ferris wheels, roller coasters, and amusement park rides, white-water rafting, hot-air ballooning, parasailing, and the like. We seek out those release experiences, but they are fleeting and short-lived. And often there is a little modicum of fear threaded into the experience.

To let go—that's one way to think about joy. There's another way, though, and it is quite the opposite. You have surely felt this feeling bubble up on an especially fine day as you are out for a walk or sitting in a comfy chair on a rainy day, reading a book. Suddenly, you stop for a moment and put down the book. Maybe you sigh. The feeling you have is one of contentment. It's not a release but the opposite—a deep engagement in the moment—and you suddenly realize that you are alive and you are well.

The world seems benevolent in a moment such as this when you are encased and nurtured by a moment in your life. In this moment there are no troubled thoughts to usher you back to the past or ricochet you into the future. You are just . . . okay. Pleased with where you are, loving the rain on the window or the sun in your face, whichever the case may be. You are not flying or doing anything outstanding or remarkable. You are just very much yourself—and ooh, that feels so good. You are—shall I say it?—blessed. You have no complaints whatsoever, and you do not want anything. You are perfectly, deliciously, rapturously . . . satisfied.

You may realize when you are in this state that this is not always your state, and you wonder why. This worry-free rhapsody comes to you when your monkey mind is quiet, when you are neither distressed about something that happened yesterday nor worrying about what's on the calendar for tomorrow. You are at rest, in neutral, and you have won this peaceful reward.

Remember it and savor it, for it will surely not last. Soon a pressing concern will jar you out of your reverie and you'll be back to business. But know that you have achieved the pinnacle of human achievement: unadulterated, ordinary, garden variety JOY!

The Happiest Places

I am always intrigued and fascinated by articles about the happiest countries on earth, aren't you? The top contenders for the happiest countries shuffle places year by year. But despite the shifts, the qualities that place these countries in contention tend to remain the same.

What makes people happy? We probably all agree that

money alone does not guarantee happiness. But the lack of it—poverty—is probably disqualifying, unless you are one of the very self-sufficient people who can flourish in spite of a very modest lifestyle. This is not the case for most people. We don't need riches, but struggling for survival saps the life out of us.

It is interesting in this vein that though the happiest countries do not necessarily have the richest citizens, they do possess a greater equality of wealth. It's hard to be happy when you have a lot but know that the people around you have little. It can't help but sully your enthusiasm for your own affluence to know that your neighbor may not have enough to eat tonight. In a society where everyone at least has enough to sustain themselves, every member can sigh in relief. We can enjoy more when we know others are not deprived.

To reach that feeling of well-being—let's call it contentment—we need to have the resources to obtain what we need as well as the security to know that we will not be harmed. The happiest countries do just that; they are concerned with the safety of their citizens, allowing them to undertake their life tasks without worry. Countries that are corrupt, undemocratic, violent, autocratic, and unstable fall at the very bottom of the happiness charts.

Social justice, fairness, protection—these are requirements for well-being, both for individuals and for society as a whole. Without them, everything else is for naught, as only with trust can one move bravely forward in life. One cannot be happy if you have to hide, conceal the truth, or disguise yourself. Freedom, therefore, is an important component of the good life.

Of course, security can come in many packages. For many people, religion offers the connection to a protective structure. Family also can provide that function, and community too, a wider, more expansive, and inclusive family substitute.

Connection to people, or a clan, friends, neighbors makes one feel part of a group, and this gives succor and fosters happiness. But humans are capable also of connecting to an idea, an occupation, a culture, or one's work. Societies that offer people opportunities to study, expand their horizons, prepare for professional work are the ones that rise to the top of the happiness list.

All of these criteria—equality, security, community, opportunity—do one thing: they remove anxiety and stress from our daily lives, thereby freeing us to relax, explore possibilities, relate to others, do creative work, and play. They are prerequisites for a good life, one that gives us the best chance to develop that boundless potential we are born with, that infinite unrealized plausibility that is diminished chip by chip by all of the negatives and disappointments, not to mention traumas we encounter in life.

Those of us who are fortunate to have been born in one of these happiest places have a much better chance of soaring. Stress is a weight that keeps us tethered to ordinariness and failure. But we all are not born lucky.

For those of us living outside these happiness zones, we can endeavor to create the conditions that exist in these places in our own sphere, relieving ourselves of stress as much as possible and creating our own happiest place right where we find ourselves. We can also work in our communities to create these conditions.

We can't all move to Finland, Denmark, Norway, Switzerland—places that have set up societies that work for most everyone. We can't, unfortunately, do much to help those in the countries at the bottom of the happiness list, mostly war-torn, hapless places with great poverty and corruption like Afghanistan, much of Africa, and a good part of the Middle East. In these places, societal problems make having a good life very difficult. That makes us very sad, and we cannot deny the pain that residents suffer.

This book is about individual potential, so we will focus on what we can do, each of us, to reduce the stress in our own lives, to be more loving, more aware, more gracious, and yes, happier. Naming the qualities that make this easier is just another way to focus on creating and nourishing joy in our lives.

Let's get on with it, shall we?

I will posit that happiness—joy—comes to us in different degrees and also in different stages. Let's start with the synonyms, as each has a slightly different cast: amusement, bliss, charm, cheer, comfort, delight, elation, ecstasy, exultation, felicity, frolic, fruition, gaiety, gladness, glee, gratification, hilarity, humor, merriment, mirth, pride, rapture, refreshment, rejoicing, satisfaction, solace, transport, treasure, wonder.

Some of these synonyms are in the category I will call pleasure: amusement, cheer, gladness, refreshment, humor, mirth, for instance. Others suggest actions or expressions of happiness or ways to achieve it: frolic, merriment, hilarity, gaiety, rejoicing. Still others suggest a heightened state of an extreme, even transformative experience: elation, ecstasy, exultation, transport, wonder. And also an achievement: as in satisfaction, fruition, gratification.

So there are as many ways to say joy as to find it. How do we find it? How does it find us?

Let's look more closely, both in the context of our daily lives and in art.

Stage One: Anticipation

We don't reach the peaks of happiness on a daily basis. For the most part, our days are filled with repetitive tasks and routine things we do without much thought to sustain and maintain ourselves, our homes, and other people we serve. We often go about these assignments without much thought or even with much consciousness, evidencing how truly routine they have become.

Who among us has not realized as we are driving a car that until a flashing moment of awareness, we have been performing this complex task unconsciously? The car has seemingly been driving itself!

Which brings us to these questions: Can there be joy without consciousness? What emotion did we experience while the car sped down the highway on automatic pilot?

To feel an emotion you can give a name to, must you be awake? We experience feelings when we are dreaming, don't we? Sometimes very intense feelings. Sometimes even joy. But dreaming is a special state. We are not literally conscious, but our brain is working and our memory of experience is driving the dream. Not so when we are in that automatic state.

If we do not recognize that we are alive and are not able to distinguish states of being, we cannot be said to feel anything, certainly not joy. If we are feeling poorly and then suddenly our state improves and we feel well, we can say we now feel something akin to happiness. Maybe we simply call it relief or refreshment, or perhaps we are thrilled that we are better and feel positively cheered. If we have suffered greatly and now no longer suffer, we may say we are elated, ecstatic, jubilant. We may twirl around and jump for . . . yes . . . joy. We are healed! We have survived!

You have probably heard people talk about the value of lowering one's expectations. Here is a different context in which you can appreciate that recommendation. Since feeling is a matter of perception, what one expects has a huge influence on how you evaluate the things that happen to you.

Let's follow through on this example of you feeling poorly and then feeling better. If you expected to get only a little better—low expectations—you would feel ecstatic if you suddenly felt well. If, on the other hand, you expected to feel immensely better and only felt a little better, you would probably be disappointed.

What we anticipate plays a very large part in how we perceive events as they come to pass. Many of us have had the experience of fantasizing about future events, especially special events, only to be disappointed when our expectations are not met. Likewise, we have experienced ordinary days with no expectations whatsoever that suddenly turn into our best, most memorable, story-worthy days, as we quite accidentally encounter something or someone very special.

How often have I given myself the admonition to not make assumptions when a cranky resistance to trying something proves to be just fear, and I surprise myself by having a really good time. Once again the Zen advice to be here now, dwell in the moment, and find joy in it shows how correct it truly is.

❧

This phenomenon is very potent in artmaking. Every artist has seen his noblest expectations crumble to dust as he projects a great plan or project into the future and then finds it is unworkable. It sounded better as an idea than it actually looks as a piece of visual art. Into the trash can it goes.

But then, remarkably, one ordinary day in the studio, a new idea is born, and it's a "three little bears" moment . . . the chair is "just right." And what does the artist feel?—exultation and JOY.

Here is a painting I did one day in thirty minutes. I had a canvas, some house paint, and I was feeling cheerful. I covered the canvas with this gray house paint, and when it dried I drew this little girl on the canvas with a crayon. She expressed what I was feeling that particular morning: lightness and self-satisfaction. I don't know why I felt so giddy—maybe it was the result of a good dream. It was still quite early in the day. The feeling came to me in the figure of this little girl holding her skirt out as little girls do when they want to show off. I grabbed some crayons I had from one of my kiddie classes and colored her party dress. Then drew her little face with charcoal.

She is not flying, as was the girl I drew as a very young art student. This girl stands fully grounded but proud of herself, just simply pleased. Time has passed, and I am pleased to see that I have returned to earth.

The joy in art is the happiness that comes when a door has opened, a through line to the artist's purpose has been made. The artist has discovered something that feels right because

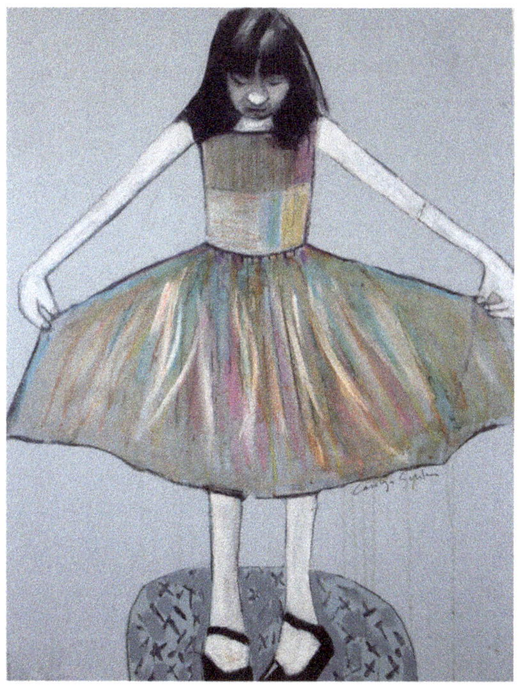

The Party Dress, 2019, Oil on canvas, 40 x 30 inches

it expresses what she hoped to say. Perhaps she did not know what that was until that very moment, but it is recognized instantly. Mission accomplished.

The motto (used as an advertisement) for playing the New York Lotto is “When you least expect it, you’re elected.” Zen wisdom in a commercial.

Stage Two: Passion

We’ve been talking about pleasure and enjoyment—the kind of joy that pops up in the course of daily living. And there is no denying it is wonderful. Yet most of us dream of a bigger happiness, a more dramatic experience—romantic, earth shattering, rocket flaring, unadulterated PASSION. The dictionary defines it as strong emotion, but not just strong—barely controllable. Wow!

We ordinarily think of passion being connected to love and, of course, lust—a wanting so intense we can almost not tolerate it; a feeling of love so powerful that it engulfs us, driving us to do crazy things—make sacrifices, prostrate ourselves. I am being dramatic, yes. But drama is an integral part of passion, is it not?

Not everyone wants passion in their lives. It can be too strong an emotion for some, too disruptive, demanding, and ego threatening. We fear we may dissolve in search of it, lose our self-control. Isn't that what the definition suggests?

Some people are more mild mannered, quieter, more appreciative of smaller joys and therefore eschew these mighty rivers of emotion, trading equilibrium for tears, upset, upheaval, even dissembling. Others rush headlong, craving these gigantic emotions and feeling deprived if their experiences are calmer and more sedate.

Which kind are you? Which way do you go?

The obvious passion is for a lover, but there are many other things humans can get passionate about: work, animals, nature, sports, travel, religion, mountain climbing, racing, chess, you name it. Oh, and art, all the arts—music, visual art, theater, film, literature—are fertile ground for passion. Creativity is a deep well for passion seekers, a veritable playground for creative types everywhere.

Is passion an altogether good thing? It's that uncontrollable aspect that causes a twinge. We all know passion can take a turn into obsession. And obsession is not healthy; it can lead to extravagance, self-indulgence, self-destructive behavior, even addiction.

We all have probably experienced times when our strong desire for something becomes impossibly disabling; the whole experience makes us feel exhausted, and we know in our heart of hearts that we must stop. I have reached that point many times in my work when my desire to capture something turns into a sickening mess, and every moment that I persist makes it more impossible to accomplish anything at all.

We never want to stop, but we must because a runaway emotion is not the state of mind and body that is likely to produce art. I say it signals the need to rest, reflect, and meditate.

We want to work like demons on our passions, but the truth is that passion, like all extreme feelings, is part of a continuum, and artmaking, like all major endeavors, requires quiet as well as noise, retirement as well as engagement, pause as well as fervor. One sets the stage for the other and puts it in context.

It's a wonderful feeling when you happen to be working and you realize you are *on*. Your senses are heightened, you are brighter and more responsive than usual. Often, for the visual artist, the stimulus is a subject that is truly captivating, something that you very much want to capture.

I draw a lot from the model and only get captivated sometimes. There is something about the position of the model, my angle of vision, the light, costumes, expression that pushes my buttons, and I really want to get it down on paper. Time is limited—I may have only a minute or five to get something down—and this time limit seems only to increase the fervor.

So to summarize, passion is a great instigator as it drives us to work hard, take chances, swing for the chandeliers, and sometimes go too far. But coupled with mindfulness, it can lead to marvelous adventures. We don't want to get rid of it, but we need to counter it at times and make it work for our art.

Here's the tricky part. We don't want to take a middle road where we manage our emotions so carefully that instead of having the highs and the lows, we live in the middle. The middle is the safe zone—the comfort zone some call it—but an artist can't live there and still expect to grow and shine. Artists are risk takers. They may not literally walk the high wire or swing on a trapeze, but in the quiet of the studio, sometimes with classical music on the radio and the dog sleeping by the door, they fly.

Leaving planet earth in their zeal to express, artists find satisfaction in their willingness to soar and the thought that they might just make it to their holy grail—personal and transcendent self-expression. Recently, I watched a team of astronauts lift off into space after twenty years of scientific study and preparation, and I thought, *Good for them. I can do that just by going to work each day.* And like those pioneers, I return to earth to relax, evaluate, and perhaps plan my next journey. It is a balancing act.

As much as I long for the moments of passion and realization, I know that rest, what we often refer to as downtime, is not only restorative, it is the propulsion that rockets us to those heights. We need one to get the other, just as the work of artmaking needs the quiet to see the noise.

Can we truly experience the calm without the storm? Or vice versa?

Stage 3: Ecstasy

I introduce you to a song by the Indian poet Rabindranath Tagore from his 1913 Nobel Prize-winning book *Gitanjali or Song Offerings*, the first book of lyrics as well as the first by a non-European to win this award. Quite a remarkable artist—writing numerous works of prose and poetry, composing music, and in later life, painting—this Renaissance man enjoyed a long and rewarding life, active in his community and as an educator. *Gitanjali* was lauded by W. B. Yeats who found these songs sublime, displaying "a world I have dreamed of all my life long." This is the very first song in the book:

> Thou has made me endless, such is thy pleasure.
> This frail vessel thou emptiest again and again,
> and fillest it ever with fresh life.
>
> This little flute of a reed thou hast carried over hills and dales,
> and hast breathed through it melodies eternally new.
>
> At the immortal touch of thy hands
> my little heart loses its limits in joy
>   and gives birth to utterance ineffable.

Thy infinite gifts come to me only on these
 very small hands of mine.
Ages pass, and still thou pourest, and still there is room to fill.

The song is a paean to joy, but this joy is over and beyond the quotidian ups of daily life. It is a calling to something momentous and wonderful, to a state we call bliss. What is the difference between happiness and bliss?

Life brings us good moments and bad, and we measure one against the other. Our moments of joy, which come to us unexpectedly—as do gifts—stand out in our memory. They offer meaning to all the moments when we are disappointed, neutral, or not feeling much at all. We call them golden moments, and they are the treasures we save for the album, even if we share them with no one. These are high points in our lives, and they define happiness.

But Tagore is giving us words that describe a state beyond happiness—the sublime state of bliss or *Nirvana*, which is endless, boundless, infinite, and filled with measureless joy. It is a connection to all that is, to the very moment, to time itself, to nature, to All.

In this connected state beyond thought, we come as close as we can to perfection, enlightenment. In Zen, the word is *Satori*—the ecstatic awakening to the meaning of life, and it comes like a lightening strike. Many stories and koans describe the moment when confusion disappears; there is a flash of realization and one suddenly experiences *kensho*—"one's true nature."

What is bliss? Can one define it in prose? I think not, but I shall try. I have left space below for you to have a go at it too.

Bliss is a state of transcendent happiness in which you find yourself totally content, wanting nothing but to be. The pulsations of joy inhabit every cell, your agreement with the moment is entire, and your union with everything that is and has ever existed is confirmed. You exist in a state that is out of time yet fully incorporated in it—unquestioning, free, light as air, and deep as the ocean. You are perfect in your singularity yet loving all. You are beyond judgment, care, worry, stress, and fear. You are in peaceful, unruffled ecstasy.

Your definition: ______________________________

____

____

____

____

____

How does bliss relate to making art? In those moments when we are in the flow of our work, we become in a sense a witness to our own activity. We may find that the art seems to be making itself, and we are observing the process, seemingly without thought. This is yet another way to describe the process of direct seeing, unencumbered creativity. It has been likened in the literature to the tying of shoes. Just as you learn to tie your shoes and never have to think about it again when performing that act, your art takes the same route, arising, without interference, from your heart and soul. Reaching the mountaintop. Orgasmic release. *Satori*. The ultimate ultimate.

An artist is always going for the ultimate: to do that one piece of art that is the very mountaintop of his or her talent and vision. We keep trying and trying. But can we ever get there?

I think of the song I used to sing as a little girl. "The bear went over the mountain. The bear went over the mountain. The bear went over the mountain. To see what he could see." And what did he see? He saw another mountain.

We may think we get there when we do something great, but secretly, we think we can do even better next time. It's that other mountain.

We can revel in the moment before we trod on, though. I've done that many times, as when I finished this painting many years ago called *The Black Veil* (see it as the lead photo in the next chapter). I loved the softness of her blue eyes under the starkness of that black veil. She's forever in my storage unit because I still love her and want to keep her near. Thankfully, as long as we are alive and able to work, there will be another mountain. And if we are really fortunate, we will climb many of them and experience that *satori* exultation multiple times in our working lives.

Joy is not a one time only, big bang explosion. The *satori* moment is a culmination, a fulfillment of feelings and thoughts that are a long time growing. But there is joy in all the steps up to the top. When we finally arrive, we can check out the view, take a deep breath of purified air, and howl out, *I did it*. And then what? Then we'll look out to the next mountain and start the climb all over again.

One last thing before we leave this subject. Let's return for a moment to the quote that begins this chapter: "Before enlightenment, chop wood, carry water. After enlightenment, chop wood, carry water." Though *satori*, or awakening, is often described as something sudden and unexpected, this quote tells us that after our enlightenment, should it arrive, we will do just what we did before. What does that mean? It means that our lives will go on as before with no apparent change. What has changed is how we view it all, but to all outward appearances, we are the same. It is like we have cleared the veil that obscured our vision, and now we see the world as it truly is. We have seen the light literally and figuratively.

The top of the mountain moment may pass into memory and we may even slip back into worry and despair. But the periodic reinforcement of these achievements and successes do have a cumulative effect. With good attention, meditation, and the like, we can hopefully step once again into the peaceful conduct of ordinary, happy daily life. And then, once again, another golden moment may arrive unexpectedly like a check in the morning mail.

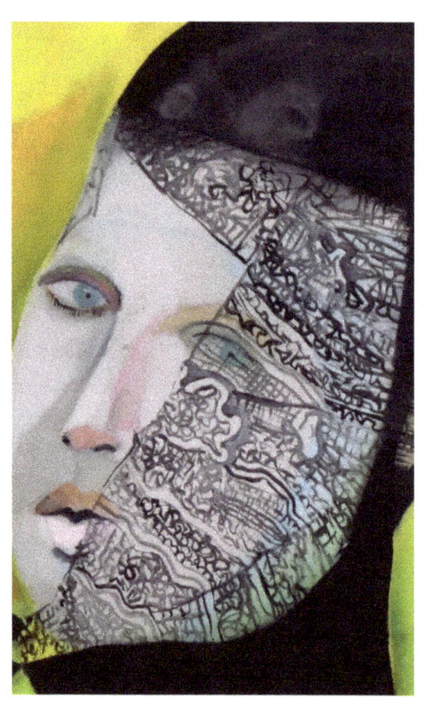

The Black Veil, 2009, Oil on canvas, 42 x 34 inches

EIGHT

Time

Do I contradict myself?
Very well then I contradict myself,
(I am large, I contain multitudes.)
—Walt Whitman, "Song of Myself," 51

I contain multitudes.
—Bob Dylan

We are visiting earth for a lifetime, during which we coexist with all that is and was and will be. We play our part as we dialogue with the universe. We make our mark and then we depart, leaving a bit of ourselves to travel on. Remember the first law of thermodynamics: energy is neither created nor destroyed.

Let's talk about time, that elusive commodity.

I love this song by Bob Dylan, written for his *Rowdy Boys* album. The song, "I Contain Multitudes," keeps resonating in my brain, that refrain playing over and over again. It is so pungent. "I contain multitudes." Yes, we all do. By the way, Dylan didn't make up this wonderful phrase. It appears earlier in a Walt Whitman poem. But Walt and Bob both did a lot of living, and though Walt thought of it first, Bob made it into music, which made me hear it. I am crediting both of them.

We are made of the stuff of the universe and the stuff of time, so much stuff that we can only use a little of it in our very short time on this trip of a lifetime. We have to be choosy, pick our faves out of the multitudes of all the stuff that ever was. It's mind-boggling.

And yet we do it. We pick out what we like, and it all adds up to who we are. Let me try and explain.

How do I attract that which I want to see and be? I posit that we put energy out into the vast universe. We send out a message, a carrier pigeon. The pigeon is my desire, my intention, what I want. And then bingo—I get that ping from outer space. The thing I am looking for. It drops into my mailbox.

Let me translate into the art sphere. I am obsessed with shapes that I identify as feminine or masculine. Say I am exploring gender in my work, and I want to create these shape-filled paintings. I have this in the back of my mind, and one day when I am visiting my mother, she offers me a treat from a bowl of fruit she has just laid out. And *whammo*, there are my shapes. I realize I don't have to hire a model after all because my shapes are in the fruit bowl, in the clouds, in my garden, everywhere I look. I asked for shapes; the universe delivered them on a platter.

This may seem like a joke (it is funny) but also a truism. We get back what we put out. This is an exchange of energy. I find what I am looking for because, well, I am looking for it. It comes to me like a present from the universe.

How do we meet someone we are attracted to? Our attraction (energy) scans the force field for the object of our affection and buzzes that ping when our paths cross. This is the dialogue with the universe I am talking about.

Bob Dylan is telling us about the gigantic library—the multitudes—we can access and download. Intention is the Dewey Decimel system that zeroes in on our choices, the specific titles out of the multitudes that become ours and we consequently become them.

Being an artist is a great way to tune into the universe because we need a lot of material. We need things that nonartists can do without. We need colors and lines and shapes and textures, themes and ideas, intensities, and surprises.

When we see a sunset, we admire it like everyone does, but we also need to deconstruct it because we might want to use it in a painting about transfiguration.

What does an angel look like? How do I express the passage of time? What does disappointment look like? These are the questions our art asks of us. These questions are not garden variety. They are hard and we need help—wherever we can get it. I will get into this topic in greater depth in the chapter on kindness. Suffice it to say here that making art demands that we look for signs from the universe ever more diligently. We would be lost without them.

So back to time. It is one of the most perplexing riddles of all. What is time? We know it is relative. As Einstein reminded us, time is all about perception: "Put your hand on a hot stove for a minute and it seems like an hour. Sit with a pretty girl for an hour, and it seems like a minute." (Excuse the sexist use of the word "pretty." Einstein may have been brilliant but male-privileged nonetheless.) What we enjoy passes quickly, and what is difficult seems to linger. Why is this exactly?

When we are doing something we like, it has our attention, we say we are *into* it. When we are bored, our attention is somewhere else; there is duality, and maybe that doubles the sense of time.

But here's the rub. Don't we want times that we enjoy to seem long and times we want to avoid short? Isn't our experience of time backward, the opposite of what we want it to be?

In my experience, this conundrum is most apparent when we are vacationing. We are going to the seaside for seven glorious days and eight sumptuous nights. Our anticipation is high, but before you can say "Jack Robinson" (my father loved that phrase), you have arrived. The days are great, the nights are great, and it is going by in a flash. By the time you get to the fourth day, you realize that you have passed the halfway mark, and this is distressing. And then, it is the night before you have to go to the airport and you think: *that was too short, next time I am vacationing for at least ten days.* It is over, alas.

Let's look at the reverse—a difficult time you want to pass quickly. A test. It seems endless. You just want to get to the last question and go home. But the time drags, and it is positively exhausting. One afternoon, and it seemed longer than that whole vacation!

Sorry, there is no fixing this, and occasions can't be switched. When we are engaged, like on a vacation, there is no time. There is sun and sea and margaritas, but no time. And when we are taking a test, there is nothing but time because there is nothing whatever to distract us from those impossible questions and our own anxiety. I guess that's why Einstein went on to tell us that "time is an illusion."

The Zen people have the only answer there is to this. They say there is only NOW, the moment we are inhabiting, which becomes the past as we say the word. But luckily, there is another NOW, and then another, and we skip from NOW to NOW like stepping stones. If this does not satisfy, I have some other consolations and also some time correctives. As the NOW keeps slipping away and the new NOW comes, and then goes too, and we cannot, no matter what we do, stop time, it can work to our benefit.

Firstly, earth keeps spinning on its orbit, the sun keeps shining, day becomes night and then again day. In other words, there is repetition. The NOWS come again and again, recognizably, and though there are always variations—thank goodness, otherwise we would be terribly bored—we are able to see patterns, stories, evolution.

You have probably heard the French phrase *deja vu*, meaning in English "seen before." This is the sensation that something happening now has happened before. It feels familiar. Less utilized is the companion phrase *jamais vu* ("never seen"), identifying something that you suspect has already happened but seems entirely new.

These phenomena color our sense of NOW and of time in general. Our lives are stories we are writing. We live in the present, but we can reread former passages. We can also imagine future episodes.

If a story is well written, it has consistency and things that occur in early chapters find their resolution in later ones. This gives us a feeling of continuity and the feeling that though our NOWS may be short, they do pile up. Our story is ongoing.

I am a lap swimmer and I generally swim the same program of seventy-two laps (about a mile) four or five times a week. I've been doing it for about twenty-five years. Let's say I swim an average of 300 laps a week for fifty weeks. So 15,000 laps a year for twenty-five years totals 375,000 laps. Each lap is seventy-five feet, so I have swum a total distance of 28,125,000 feet. Each swim takes about forty-five minutes, so multiply that by 5,208 swims, and I've swum for 234,375 minutes or 3,906 hours or 162.7 days.

It's not really that much time when you break it down. But it is interesting because I have such a vivid sense of time while I am swimming, and it varies quite a bit. Sometimes that forty-five minutes seems endless and other times it's like nothing at all. It all depends on my state of mind and body. Let's examine this.

When does the time drag on? When I am tired, have an ache, when I am not swimming well, when I have something else I would prefer doing, when I am hungry, when I want to lie down, when I am impatient. Aha!

And when does the time pass quickly? When I feel good, am frisky, nothing aches. When my mind and body are just putt- putt- puttering along—*poof*, five laps go by. When I am swimming well, I feel like a fish, and am really present. When this happens and I complete my swim, I feel like I could swim another seventy-two. I say, *that was a good one!*

Once again, the Zen attitude shows the way. The difference in my perception of time is my level of egoless engagement. When I am tired, impatient, and hungry, my attention is distracted. I am in the pool, but my mind is somewhere else. I have expectations, wants, needs. On the other hand, when I can relax into my swim, I am in the moment; my mind is alive, but it is not interrupting my swim. I am truly in the flow, occupying the moment.

What does this tell us? A lot, I think. To commit to the moment, to embrace it, to be where we are and enjoying it to the max, we need to be our best selves, which includes getting sufficient rest and nutrition, relaxing into whatever we are doing, and foregoing past concerns and future expectations. Could it be that it takes preparation to be in the moment? Is that a contradiction? This hearkens back to our discussion of spontaneity and what it means to be free-spirited.

To be in the moment does not mean to be without thought, an airhead wandering in a forest. To the contrary. What is more liberating than to be strong and healthy, vigorous and in possession of all your human abilities?

With full power, we abide in the moment. As the Zen monks admonish: ***When you are swimming, swim. When you are sleeping, rest. When you are hungry, eat.*** A Zen officiant named Yun-men said, "In walking, just walk. In sitting, just sit. Above all, don't wobble." Simple?

Most assuredly so. Yet so difficult. Perhaps it is those "multitudes we contain." They keep popping up all the time, often at the most inconvenient times. You may have heard mention of it as the "monkey mind," the chattering interference that plays in our consciousness and interrupts everything.

When you are doing something, be aware of where your attention really is. If it is not with you, bring yourself back like you do when you are meditating and your mind wanders—gently repeat your mantra or return to your breath. Slip back into now.

This is an opportune moment to talk about meditation. Certainly one of the key pillars of Zen practice, the purpose of meditation is to help us sit in the moment and calm the multitudes.

You may think of meditation as something you do when you

sit still, close your eyes, and repeat a phrase or watch your breath. That is certainly the classic pose. But you can carry the meditating mind with you into the swimming pool, on a hike, into almost any activity, and certainly into the art studio. (Remember what I said earlier about sitting in my rocking chair.)

When I am swimming and I feel impatient, I implore myself to feel the water, to become a fish in its habitat, and to relax. When I am walking and find myself worrying about something I have to do tomorrow, I gaze at the flowers on my path to return me to today.

Making art is a pretty dreamy task most of the time. It is one of the activities that, by its very nature, engenders absorption and engagement. Swimming is pleasurable and uses the entire body, but artmaking engages even more of our organism. If you have had the experience of working at your art and then suddenly realizing that hours have gone by and you have been so involved that time has just evaporated, then you know of what I speak. You may not necessarily have created a masterpiece in this beautiful reverie you have experienced, but no matter, you have had a splendid afternoon in which you lived the moment to its fullest.

But this is not always the case. It is so very easy to get off track when we are making art, to get distracted, side-tracked, pulled in more directions than our intention laid out. What to do then?

The answer? Focus. Meditation may sound like a mysterious practice, but it is really just this: focusing the mind on the present. The discordant notes on the canvas are the physical manifestations of the chattering monkey mind. With focus, we can know which ones belong to our inspiration and which ones have dropped in from outer space. (By the way, some of the latter may wisely be salvaged for another artwork where they appropriately may live.) With focus, we can return to the sanctuary of the present moment, and calm will reign again in the studio.

The following sections break time into what we are taught to think of as its three divisions: past, present, and future. These are artificial divisions, but they have significance in this book. Zen says—and we know—that we live in only one of these spheres: the present. But what can we make or discern of the other two?

Many of us, myself included, wear a watch and are acutely tuned to the passing of time. How much time we have to do something, how much time we have wasted, how much time we have left to live. Time weighs on us and troubles us, molds our thinking, and shapes our perception of events.

I will elaborate on this, but before I do, I will posit the following: we live only in the present; therefore, what do the past and future represent?

The past represents our gathering of skills and experiences—that is its great value. It has given us the multitudes, our character, temperament, idiosyncrasies, propensities, knowledge—all in preparation for now. We have collected so much, made so many mistakes, done so much that it is all quite staggering and impossible to calculate. Its value is that it has brought us to this moment when we can make another plan, another choice as we add yet more knowledge to our collection, to our being.

Then we have the present, which is life, movement, and possibility realized. It is our soul in action and it is everything . . .

What, then, is the future? An idea, perhaps? The future is our intention and our hope. It does not exist except in this present in which it is imagined. When we arrive at it, it has vanished, having moved quickly from present to the library that is the past.

Now we will take the microscope and look more closely into time. Let's get on with it.

The Past

Einstein told us that time is an illusion, but we weren't born yesterday, were we? We have lived and we know it. We have a memory, a consciousness of things that have happened to us and of places we have been. We have what is called muscle memory too. We remember how to swim and ride a bicycle, and do the myriad things we find we are able to do. We are able to use words and make sense out of them, to write, to think.

Yes, this is all true, but how whole are these memories? There are some people who have such remarkable recall that they can remember what they had for dinner on March 15, 1996, and every other day as well. We call these people savants and this ability is extremely rare. But even these savants have fragmented memories. They might remember a few salient facts about a particular day just as ordinary people can remember facts about special days, like their wedding day, or a day when they had a terrible accident. But even then, the memory is scant when you consider all the many things that happened to us.

Memories we have of the past become stories. After we have told these stories many times to others—to prove to them that we had a past and that it was real, not, as Einstein tells us, an illusion—the stories seem just like stories, and we're not even sure they actually happened. As we tell them, we embellish aspects, leave out facts, and we transform the memory into a better and better tale. It becomes less and less true as time goes on.

Think of your dreams. Elements of your supposed past get all mushed together as you lie in your bed and dream. Where are you? you wonder. It looks like your childhood bedroom, but why is it next door to the house you live in now? And who is that person who says she's your mother? She looks like the woman who swam in the adjacent lane of the swimming pool you were in yesterday. All of the memories mix together, regardless of when they occurred. Everything is a jumble and a mess.

But wait a minute, you say, *I know it happened, it must*

have. Was I dreaming? The truth is that whatever it was, it isn't available now. The only thing we absolutely can be sure about is now. Everything else is a story. As the Zen saying goes: "eternity is nothing other than right now."

Here's the good news. Though the past is a jumble, you are not. What you learned in the past has come along with you into the now. It is available. The things you said are not, but the words you used to say them with are. The mixtures of paint you made are history, but you still can reconstruct the formulas. It is in your hands, your eyes, it is YOU!

I sometimes think of the past as a bank vault. There's a lot in there—those stories, of course, and a huge volume of images. Think of all you have seen in your many years on earth. Google images has nothing on you. You have seen with childhood eyes and adult eyes, from so many perspectives, and in so many environments. Your bank is so full that you already have everything you need to do the clarifying and reshuffling you will be doing when you make your own images.

Let's call the past what it is—an audition or dress rehearsal for the big show. And when is the show? This very moment. Everything in the past got you to this place and time. And thank you very much; it's done its job.

So here I am standing at the easel in the same position I have been in so many times in the past—at least I think so. My arm has moved to make mixtures on the palette that I have made thousands of times before—at least I think so. I sweep my arm across the canvas with reminiscent vigor and direction—at least I think so. I remember how to paint—at least I think so.

This is good, right? There is continuity. Like all beings, we are creatures of habit. But then, you ask, how can I be in the moment? How can we act in the moment when all our past experience engraved on our recollection is encouraging us to repeat, repeat, repeat. How do we, in other words, remain fresh as artists?

This is a frequently asked question. Doesn't the past determine how we act in the moment? How can we be in the moment with everything that has happened before directing our thoughts and movements?

I think I have the answer, at least as it refers to making art. To remain fresh, to be present, we take what we have learned—it's there, we can't get rid of it—but we don't let it get in the way. Our desire to be present overrides what we have done before. Our desire to be new and to be our best directs us to take what we know to the next level. We remember the mixture, but we ask: *How can I make it glow more, be softer, express passion? How can I make that organic shape I always make be stronger, more gravitational, bolder?*

In other words, in every moment, we move to exceed what has proceeded it, to be more present, more alive, more loving. We use the past, but it doesn't command us. It's good information, but we can do better.

This is the way of nature too. Progression. Growth. Every year a tree grows a branch. The bird flies from tree to tree. It doesn't have to remember on which branch it landed. It doesn't matter. All that is important is that it has remembered how to fly.

You can fly, too, once you let the past just be, let it come back to you in the jumble of dreams, but concentrate on what you're doing right now and how you can enjoy it more, feel it more, be it more. How can I be original this very second? Oh, yes, I'm still me, but this is a new me. Every moment is another chance to be a new and improved you, to make a new and improved work of art. All you need is to let the past fly away like that little bird.

Present

Ah, you have arrived. To the present. Presence is a synonym for life. You are here. Alive.

I am in my present writing these words, and you are in your present reading them. Isn't that just the best? I don't know about you because I am not with you. I am like the light from the star that you are seeing now that left that star a million years ago. But it doesn't matter, does it? Remember—eternity is right now.

We are both in our presents. I'll tell you how I am feeling. The words are coming out of my fingers like I am talking to you. I imagine you reading them. We are connected. I think it is just a wonder that I can share my thoughts with you like this. I hope you are liking them and relating. I hope you are sitting in a comfortable place and feeling content. I hope my words make you feel relaxed and hopeful.

It is afternoon, exactly 4:21 on March 31, 2021. I am lying on my bed with my laptop on my knees. It is a warm day, about 80 degrees. The room is exceedingly quiet. The window behind me is open, and a tiny breeze is finding its way in. My little dog is waiting for me to take her on her 4:40 stroll.

I am as happy as I can possibly be, thanks to you. The fact that I am able to take these words and send them out into the universe and that someday they will bounce into your eyes, well, that is a dream come true.

What are you happy about that is revealed in this moment? Say it out loud. The vibrations will land somewhere—I promise you.

We are present. We are having a direct experience on this day in our lives, this moment in this day. As I write this, I am closing my eyes and taking a deep breath. You do the same. We have meditated together.

I want to celebrate. I am going to write a haiku to celebrate. Okay? It is now 4:29, and I begin.

I present to you
my present
Give me yours
We are together
now.

That is it for now. It is 4:33. Time to walk the dog. See you again soon.

Future

This brings us to what comes next, or might be coming—our future, the great unknown.

The future is more of a fiction than the past. As I explained earlier, the future is our land of hope, a place we conjure with the utmost emotion. It is important to us because we think it is the place where we can redeem our past disappointments. It is the place where all is corrected, and since we don't really know what is going to happen, we can paint the rosiest, most favorable picture.

In this futureland only good things happen. No one suffers or gets sick, or god forbid, dies. No one gets pimples or trips and falls, especially ourselves. It is this way because we get to design it. The problem is that we can't account for all the things we cannot control, like viruses that turn into pandemics, people falling asleep at the steering wheel, and the like, and then all the misjudgments and mistakes we ourselves are bound to make.

In 2021 I applied for a fellowship that I was really hoping to receive. But I soon learned that I was one of 220 applicants, and I was not one of perhaps three who were chosen. The administrators of the grant sent a letter to all the losers telling them they were not chosen and also saying that the persons who were selected met the criterion of being "cohesive cohorts."

Oops. If I had only known that I needed to be one of those, I might have framed my application in an entirely different way. But that phrase would never in a million years have pierced my consciousness, so there was no way I could have known.

In that present moment many months ago, I was clueless. Therefore, I failed to script my future effectively. But really, no one can. "If I only knew" has got to be one of the most oft-repeated phrases defining failure. But so is "live and learn."

The next time I write a fellowship application, I may take into account that being a "cohesive cohort" might be a factor and write that into my application. The thing is, I may still lose because in that next grant opportunity, working alone might be the winning strategy. Go figure.

So how do we handle this whole future business. I posit that the greatest thing about the future is that it is a fiction. It can be anything. It is the land of endless possibility, which may or may not be realized. Given that, I can still do what I can in this present moment to increase the possibilities for x and decrease them for y. What I can't do is make them really come to pass.

We just don't know enough and, certainly, we have no control over the forces of the universe we abide in. There's so much going on in the present that we don't know anything about. How can I, a literal grain of sand in the scheme of things, exert my will over anything?

Intention. That's the word. That's all I can really do. Set an intention. Then just live in all the present moments. Let's explore what this means.

Remember the carrier pigeon? Sending messages to the universe in an attempt to make something happen? That message is your intention. What you are really doing is programming yourself to act in a certain way, to take certain paths and not others in trying to fulfill your own hopes.

It's obvious how we do this with big decisions such as going to school to take a particular course, joining a chess club to meet other chess players, that kind of thing. We put ourselves where we need to be to affect happenstance, like meeting a compatible friend or lover.

Let's look at how we create the outcomes we desire in art. When I made the painting that appears on the cover of my book *The Creative Path*, I decided to ask my then teenage niece to pose for me. She was seventeen at the time.

I am a figurative artist, and my subjects are primarily women. My niece was in that time of life when she was blossoming, and it occurred to me that this could become the subject of the work. For me, a portrait needs to express a larger theme, which in this case I designated as the flowering of youth. This, then, became my intention.

I made the canvas, a rather large one as I felt I needed the space to create not only the figure but a feeling of place. It is important that the artist feel excited about the subject, and this subject elated me! Imagine, a beautiful young girl in a sea of flowers!

Today, in my present, I am beginning work on another subject that interests me; this one not as idyllic as the painting of my niece but equally as intriguing. It is a large painting of a woman sitting in a Raggedy Ann doll kind of pose. I am excited thinking about it! It expresses something else about womanhood than the other work, something about the burden placed on women to be the doll, the object of male fantasy as she sits in a pose of resignation.

This woman/doll who I will conjure (I do not always have live models) exists in some form in my mind in this present moment. The actual woman who will be painted is in the future. She is my hope, my imagining. But in a few days, as she enters the studio for real, as she is born on the canvas, she will morph from an imaginary future woman to an immediate present one. The thing is—she will not be the same woman, the one I imagine in this present moment. That present—days from now—will make her different, and it will also reveal something about me and my reflections on women in general.

This is what makes me want to paint her. If I knew what she would be, where would the fun be? I ask you: do you really want to know the future?

Of course the answer is a resounding no. It's fun in the present to imagine the future and even to cast an intention about what we want it to be. But then we want it to be a surprise! We are curious beings, aren't we?

Wasted Time

We are all familiar with the concept of wasted time. In order to have such a thing, we believe that some of our time is positive—

we're using our time productively and something is happening—and some of our time is negative—we're not using time wisely, and it is therefore useless, a filler, what we refer to in drawing and painting as negative space.

In visual art, negative space is another term for air. We are positing that there are objects that are solid and identifiable and between them there is nothing, a negative, just air, which doesn't count.

Art teachers tell students to observe the negative space when they are drawing, to be cognizant of the shape of these "nothing" spaces so as to better define and therefore draw correctly the positive objects. But there is another way to see this picture, and this is how I explain it to my students: Imagine that there is no negative space and that everything is positive. The air is not a nothing, it is a definite something. Yes, it has a shape, and I notice it. But I see the whole scene of what is before me not as a collection of objects surrounded by a void, but as a tapestry where everything, every note of color and texture, is positive. Moreover, all the molecules that comprise these notes are connected. It is all one picture. There is nothing that is less. Nothing that is separate. Nothing that is wasted.

Imagine you could see time as a tapestry. Then you can see that the quiet, in-between times when nothing is happening, what many people call wasted time, is nothing of the kind. These quiet moments are important and necessary threads in the tapestry of your life, just as beautiful and essential as the threads of the most memorable event times. It's all equal, all part of the big picture.

Now imagine how this idea of a tapestry will impact the way you make a picture or create any piece of art, a symphony, a novel, or a play? Or the way you look at any assignment? Or how you weigh a day or an experience? Unfragmented. As a whole.

Now looking at a work of art as a viewer, you can do the same thing. You may not realize it, but your eye travels around a painting and searches for the way in and the way out. I am very conscious of this "path" when I am composing a canvas.

As a viewer, you can find and follow this path; find the way to enter the work and then to travel around it and exit. There is a map there. It is not marked, but look with consciousness and you will find it.

You can look at any work of art and find that all the elements—foreground, background, object, air—are equally important and that the success or failure of the work depends on all of these. Perhaps you can even see a portrait, with just the distinct figure and background, as a whole; with the pixels of paint in the so-called background having the same importance as the light on the nose.

This will surely increase your appreciation of art. Likewise, I daresay that using this approach and getting the big picture in life generally can have an equally beneficial reward. In my opinion, moving your point of view back far enough that you can see your life as a tapestry—rather than a bunch of separated, good and bad events, is the key to fulfillment. Imagine that your vision for life that continues to be painted every moment, and every element has equal significance.

We are all part of the fabric of the tapestry that is earth, and all our moments are part of the tapestry that is our life. Doesn't that picture make you feel wonderful? It's a great big affirmation that everything we are and do is meritorious as it is part of the whole. The grandest moments come by virtue of all the ordinary ones. It's a package deal, as they say.

Time and Art

The fact that all this fun and adventure will some day end lingers in the back of our consciousness in a little room we dare not enter. The name on the door is death.

This seemingly empty dark room colors everything we do and are. We keep its existence at bay most of the time, but sometimes, most likely on the occasion of a special moment, it pierces us. There is an end, and this moment will not come again. Whatever are we to do?

What pops into my mind is to take the moment that you wish would never end and . . . write a poem about it. Turn it into art. Why? Art is the only way we can take our truth, the complexity of who we are in this moment and what we are experiencing, and transform it into an entity that will not, cannot die.

This thing we create called art is our only messenger, our carrier pigeon to new worlds. Others around us will also die, even the youngest among us.

Art is a way to fertilize the time we will never have. To give birth to a work of art is to allow your spirit to take flight into the world that is beyond your very life, to give it to the next generation, and the next.

Through art, we live on. Imagine it. The poem you write today is a little bird that may alight on a human branch five hundred years hence and inspire that being to create another work of art in a medium you never could have foreseen, for an audience another five hundred years down the road, maybe even on another planet.

So do not be sad. Savor every moment and live your life to the fullest. And if you would like, fly. Make art and turn your moment into eternity.

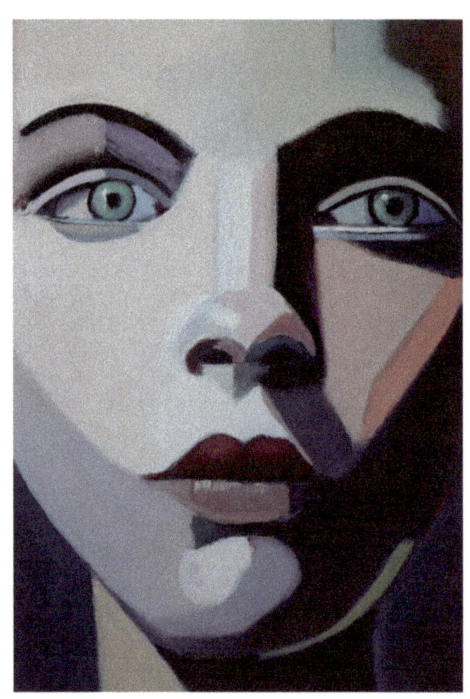

Marina, Oil on canvas, 40 x 30 inches

NINE

Beauty

"To love beauty is to see light."

—Victor Hugo

Nature

When I set out to write this book, I did not plan to include this topic. But one day when I was out on a walk, on a particularly beautiful early spring day, I noticed all the new growth on the many plants and trees blooming in my neighborhood. I was struck with the multifarious display of the bushes and flowering trees just in this small area, and I got to thinking about the magnificence of nature on planet Earth.

Astounding in complexity, variety, and exquisiteness, nature is the ultimate measure of what we call beauty. No man-made object, regardless of how innovative and lovely, can compare with the sheer magnificence of the natural world. Can any human invent something more ferociously beautiful than a tiger? More delicate than an orchid? More mysterious than the iridescence of water? More powerful than a redwood tree? More inspiring than a sky lit with the first rays of day?

All of our concepts about beauty, I believe, arise from our perceptions of the natural world. Everything we know and have seen come from our home—planet Earth. We are blessed with an incredibly splendid environment of mountains, valleys, bodies of water in every shape and size, deserts and wetlands, and prairie, cliffs, and islands, meadows filled with flowers, waterfalls and pools, and great expansive vistas of water and land and sky. These fill our eyes and define our criteria for what is beautiful.

What makes these visions possible? Light, which gives us color, transparency, subtleties of mist and fog, bright sunshine, and shade. Also air, the atmosphere, that softens everything we see, taking all hint of harshness away. You have see it all, haven't you? You must have noticed the bolt of light through the clouds that beamed down to Earth and thought: *How beautiful! It must be God speaking to us with that beam of light.* Or you awakened early one morning to catch the nascent enlightenment as the sun rose, or you sat spellbound in the evening as it blazed the day's final glory.

Sunrise. Sunset. Sunshine. Our eyes fill with light as it filters through air, and all of the myriad vistas are illumined for our pleasure. It is a joy to open one's eyes to the light of day, isn't it? This is undeniable.

As artists, we speak of the elements of art: light, color, line, shape, form, space, and texture. These are our building blocks in the construction of a work of art. And from where do our ideas about these elements come? From nature, of course, from what we see and feel in our world. Even the things we imagine might exist on other planets are related to the familiar things we have observed on ours. Maybe the rocks are more plentiful or sharper. Maybe the land is dryer or has an unusual texture. But these imagined things are related to the actual things on Earth that we have been looking at all our lives.

Earth is our laboratory, our school, and the source of all visual information. Whether we imitate nature, transform it, or utterly reimagine it, if we didn't have the "it," we would have no context, no starting place.

Mother Earth we have named her and she is the midwife of our creativity. As an artist, the delicacy and fragility of a flower guides my hand and leads me to apply my line oh so tenderly.

Likewise, my whole body contributes to my stance when I describe something firm or hard.

Nature not only tells us how things look or appear but how they feel, and indirectly, how we feel about them. Let me give you a few examples.

Most of the earth is covered by water, and let's face it, we humans worship water. Not only is it life-sustaining, it is life itself. So many of us want to be near water, so much so that living near or overlooking water is reserved for the elites among us. The rest of us flock to the beach, riverside, or lake whenever we possibly can. The word vacation is practically synonymous with water, and we seek to be near it for our most important occasions and celebrations.

The painter Claude Monet retired to his glorious pond in Giverny where he made endless variations of the water and waterlilies that floated there, until it all morphed into a glorious swirl of color and texture. He was so moved with the beauty that he was in a reverie.

Monet was not alone. Artists through the centuries have been fascinated with the mysteries of water. It is a substance that absorbs and reflects the light in a most fascinating way, so you cannot say what the color of water is at all. It can be bluish or greenish or grayish or brownish or a million shades, depending on the weather and the quality of the light.

And not only water. Air too. The painter William Turner was a great example of one so carried away by the fact that the earth has an atmosphere that he became a veritable storm chaser, painting the sky and sea in the rain, snow, and fog. He adored the soupy mess, objects appearing and then disappearing into the mist.

How do sculptors get their ideas about shape? From the incredible array of shapes that nature delivers: rocks, mountains, land masses, creatures large and small, trees, bushes, clouds.

Wherever you look there are new pieces of sculpture of living matter. And inhabiting these shapes are the ones we imagine. Haven't you seen a rabbit in a cloud? A pile of rocks you were convinced was a human? The breasts of a woman in a mountain vista? Of course you have. In all the formations of our world, we find an infinite number of other forms, beings, critters. And it all comes from what we see everyday.

Many of the objects we create are conjured with the imprint of our most favorite faces and forms. If you haven't already noticed, have a gander at how fire hydrants resemble dogs and tools look like birds and all manner of things; cars, mops, shopping bags, houses, boxes, you name it happen to sport two eyes, a nose, and a mouth. Why do you think people find saints in sandwiches and pizza pies? We see ourselves and our world in everything.

Because we are conscious, because we have emotions, because we think, we are able to take our visual canvas, planet Earth, and manipulate it for our own purposes and enjoyment. Not only can we imitate it, we can comment on it, and we do just this to make art. We will discuss that in our next section. Before we do, though, let us remind ourselves that when we consider what is beautiful, the genesis of our visual opining is nature. Nature is our source.

The Buddhists have a word for something they call "suchness"—*tathata*. It refers to the essence of things beyond words. I believe that one of the reasons humans are disposed to make art is to articulate this suchness. A billion words cannot describe the beauty of a rainbow fish flitting in the shallow aquamarine waters or the light streaming down a valley floor, but perhaps a daring artist standing alone in his studio can give it a try; he is thinking he must. He will not succeed, but the trying honors the beauty and points the way for the rest of us.

Beyond Nature

I am a visual artist and make static images and sculptural forms. But I cannot leave this subject of the beauty of nature without discussing natural processes, which, if possible, are even more wondrous than the structure of natural forms.

I am an artist, not a scientist, but I understand how studying the mystery of any minute aspect of any one of the millions of remarkable processes that occur in nature could command one's attention for a lifetime: reproduction and birth in all its forms, ecosystems, life under the sea, animal behavior, galaxies, time, gravity, and all the other forces that command us. The way nature works is so utterly amazing that I do not have words to discuss it.

My meager testament to all of this is in this description I wrote of the sterling 2020 documentary called *My Octopus Teacher*, directed by Pippa Ehrlich and James Reed, documenting a year filmmaker Craig Foster spent forging a relationship with an octopus. Here's my reaction to that film:

Thoughts/Inspirations after Viewing The Octopus Teacher

I recently viewed a quite remarkable film called *The Octopus Teacher*. My initial reaction when it was suggested by a friend was to demur— *an octopus movie . . . not exactly my cup of tea*. But, not wanting to be close-minded, I agreed to watch. And how very glad I did as this was not only a beautifully photographed film and mesmerizing in its vision, it had much to say about big ideas—the meaning of life, the joy of life, and so on.

It is difficult to describe in words the emotional impact of the film as the phantasmagorical vision of the undersea universe depicted is so essential to the understanding of the film's message. But I will try.

I learned that the octopus is a marvel, a practically liquid creature referred to in the film as a mollusk, which has the ability to change its appearance in myriad ways. It is so fluid that it is difficult to draw the actual shape of this being in my mind. It seems not to have a solid shape and has the ability to blend into its environment in fascinating ways. In one incarnation, seeking to escape danger, it draws to itself various detritus of the sea—shells and the like—so it becomes totally disguised and unrecognizable to predators. How utterly clever—and we humans think we are smart—and how totally unexpected.

The octopus has a relatively short life span, only about a year, but what a year it is! Spending lots of time hiding in its den, it dares to venture out into its splendidly ornate environment as it dodges all manner of fearsome enemies, particularly the dastardly sharks. In one riveting scene, we see the octopus's dodge partially fail as the beast manages to crop a piece of one of octie's arms. Will it survive? we wonder, worrying the creature's hiding mechanisms may have been for naught?

And to our great reward, we discover that not only does our friendly sea denizen survive, it slowly and determinedly grows the arm back. We are not surprised that revivification is one of its many talents, and we root for this brave being to make it.

The marine scientist responsible for bringing the octopus to film becomes besotted, not only with its marvelousness, but with the astounding trust the creature exhibits as it slowly becomes cognizant of the human interloper and decides it is friendly and worthy of attention. We get a sense of the tiny scale of the octopus as it ultimately rests lovingly on the chest and in the hand of the man.

In the end, the scientist has to witness the demise of the octopus once it has fulfilled its purpose and procreated the sea with descendants, most of whom will not survive. This is the octopus's destiny, and it accepts it with the courage and beauty with which it has lived its yearlong lifetime. So poignantly, the scientist admits not only his respect but his love for the tiny animal.

What has the scientist learned? What have we, the witnesses, learned? The film has reinforced important understandings: the magnificence of our world; the unfathomable complexity of its properties and living creatures; the gift we have been given to experience, see, enter, plunge, and fall into its beauty; the meaning of the life cycle; and how our lives are given meaning because we have so little time to be in it, some day we must say goodbye. The film speaks of tenderness and kindness and humility. We are wondrous creatures, surely, but we are not the only ones or even the most important. Our joy is to be just part of this extravaganza we call home, to wiggle, bask, jump for joy that we made it, that we're here and we're savoring it all, every day, every way, because we can.

Finding joy in nature, both in its appearance and processes, is tremendously important in our lives, but for us as artists, nature is a springboard for our practice. How we turn this joy into art is the question here, and I want to applaud those who are able to accomplish it in motile forms like filmmaking.

Expression

We humans are amazing creatures, and we continue to try to surpass what is given to us, but we cannot. Probably the closest we get to imitating or trying to match the beauty of nature is with our art. In an attempt to create beauty with visual art, artists often chase after spectacular examples of nature to try to manufacture a reasonable facsimile. A sunset, for example, or a splendid landscape with flowing waters, a beautiful young woman at the pinnacle of innocent charm, or a bouquet of flowers—things we all recognize to be extraordinarily beautiful. These subjects continue to be popular as artists never cease trying to master them. Why do artists do this? What motivates them to try to imitate the beauty of nature? Isn't it enough that we can see it and admire it? What is it about the re-creation that is necessary?

It's quite simple—artists think it can be accomplished and that they will be the ones to do it. And some are exceptional at it, getting oh so close. In a sense, they bring us closer to the beauty of nature because they put a frame on it and hang it on a wall. That may compel us to take a serious look. But, in my opinion, as I have said before, the art, even if spectacular, never surpasses the real thing.

One of the things artists do accomplish is to officially mark what engages them the most, and this forces the viewer to focus closely on a segment of the big picture nature provides. The artist is distilling a particular beauty out of the vastness for the viewer's study and delight. This may, perhaps, help all of us to appreciate the whole even more.

Artists can take what they see, admire, love, worship even, and then ask: *What is it that I, this particular human on this particular day in my life, have to say about this sunset, this beautiful girl, this bouquet of flowers? Okay, I won't imitate it, but I will comment on it, tell others what moves me. How will I tell you? With what I choose to highlight, with the colors I choose, the way I move my brush, the shapes I make.*

So what am I really doing? I am telling you not about the sunset but about the me that admires the sunset, and not just the me, in general, but the me right now in this very moment. So there is really no sunset on the canvas at all; what you see is me loving the sunset. That's my art.

Art is expression. We use nature to guide and inspire us, but we don't make nature. We can't. Did you think we were God? No, we are commentators.

Being a commentator is no small feat though. It is important. When history brought humans to the stage of consciousness where they realized that the job of artists is not to imitate nature, but to comment on it, there was an explosion, a Big Bang in awareness. Artists were liberated because if you are not copying something, but imagining or commenting . . . well . . . the sky doesn't have to be blue, and a flower doesn't have to have a stem, and a woman can have two faces, and, well, anything is possible. Isn't it?

There's no reason whatsoever to try to compete with God or nature. God/nature can make flowers. I, the artist, can make rivers of paint that may be flowery, but they're not flowers; no insect is about to come calling. I have a brain and a heart stocked with feelings and ideas. I can take my perception of the flower, extract this and add that, and apply it in a new way. I can make something fantastic and eye-opening, if I choose.

The painting I did of my niece Alexandra, called *Alexandra in Bloom,* was just that—an experiment in floweriness. She was seventeen at the time, and I imagined her just becoming a woman—blooming, if you will. I took the conceit of painting her on a flowered couch in a flowered dress with a bouquet of flowers on a nearby table. Not only was Alexandra blooming but everything in the painting was as well. This made making the painting interesting as well as a visual challenge for me.

I like to do an exercise with students where I write words on little pieces of paper and put them into a jar and have the students select one and then paint it. The words are usually not nouns because if I wrote "chair," the exercise would be too easy. I usually write adjectives like dank, evanescent, jazzy, hysterical—words that don't conjure up a particular image at all. Any subject can be rendered in a dank, evanescent, jazzy, or hysterical way: a fish, a bouquet of flowers, or even an abstract image that doesn't represent an actual object. Students may seem dumbfounded at first but soon recognize that their creativity may be charged by answering the call of this difficult assignment.

I have it in mind to return to the flower motif in another work, one in which the floweriness creates even more of a dizzying tapestry of shapes so that the figures and background are less clearly defined and so blend. Artists often engage in a game of telephone where they start with one idea and continue to modify it, taking the last attempt as inspiration for the next. That is a fundamental way an artist can develop a body of work, and it is fascinating for the viewer to follow artists' tracks as they look at the works in sequence.

Expressiveness—that is what we are after. It happens when an artist puts the personal into her subject. This gives the viewer not a neutral object but the object—even if it is abstract—touched by a human heart and brain. From the initial selection of the subject itself and the artist's angle of vision, then through all the steps she takes, the artist reveals what is important to her and has germinated her expressive treatment.

Though the criteria for beauty are often defined as some aspect of attractiveness depicted through proportion or symmetry, or a partiality for regularity, color, lightness, delicacy, etc., these have cultural determinants that are constantly changing. In one era, time, and place, pulchritude is defined as round and soft; in another, thin and long. So these criteria are in effect meaningless, and expressiveness is not limited to cultural or temporal relativity. It is eternal.

When we recognize a work of art as expressive, we may perceive it as beautiful or ugly or neither. What we say is that the art is effective, purposeful, or meaningful, imparts feeling and thought, and unequivocally sends a message. Whether that message is pleasant or nasty is irrelevant. Expressiveness overrides beauty and is a loftier achievement.

Nature is beautiful in its utter variety, complexity, interrelatedness, and the way every piece is part of the whole. In its systems, functions, and purpose, all of the forms in nature are intertwined, and this order is beauty incarnate. Some think of the order—nature—as the divine.

Words fail in our celebration of nature. Again, I fall back on the Buddhist concept of suchness—that which cannot be expressed in words.

Ugliness

We have talked about beauty, but what about its opposite? Is there such a thing as ugliness? If beauty is expressiveness, authenticity, and truth, its opposite, ugliness, logically must be emptiness and falsification. In the real world there is much that we find ugly: hatred, bigotry, cruelty, war, disrespect, corruption—all are destructive in their effect and fall into the category of ugliness.

Is there a corollary in art? Do the ugly things in life find their way onto the canvas?

We all form impressions of what is normal, neutral, expected. When there is deviance from that standard, it disturbs us, and we may think of these aberrations as ugly. Too small, too large, twisted, distorted, malformed—these are common words associated with ugliness. But variation, though it can be alarming or discomfiting, is not ugliness. It is merely unfamiliar.

We must make a distinction in art between expressions that may be extreme and those that may be unfamiliar, between works that are false and devoid of expressive qualities and works that intentionally and purposefully distort from the norm. The former may be works that are expressive, while the latter we classify as exploitative or dishonest. There is no ugliness in art that shows us painful realities and moves us. It is the purpose of art to reveal truth regardless of the subject. Truth revealed, whatever the appearance, is beautiful.

These two lines were written enigmatically at the end of John Keats's famous poem "Ode on a Grecian Urn": "Beauty is truth, truth beauty. That is all / Ye know on earth, and all ye need to know." This concept is not universally accepted. The poet TS Eliot said these lines were meaningless. Ian Stewart, a mathematician who wrote ***Why Beauty is Truth: A History of Symmetry***, agreed with Keats, but for a different reason. He found symmetry to be at the heart of beauty (which I find limiting), but also concluded that "everything false is ugly."

Everyone sees this concept in a different way. Let me explain my truth. Please use it to find and express yours.

In my thinking, the path to beauty or ugliness begins with intention. If you come from a place of love and your intention is to express what you feel and think, to reveal your heart, mind, and soul, and manifest it in art, regardless of what others may think, you are abiding in beauty. If, instead, your intention is to aggrandize, falsify, impress, fool, or influence others, regardless of what you feel and think, you are in the realm of ugliness.

Still, if you ask a hundred artists whether they are trying to create beautiful works of art, most will say yes. My teacher, Norman

Raeben, wrote his ten commandments of art, and the last one was very difficult to comprehend. It seemed to go against everything he was teaching us. As we struggled to make beautiful drawings and paintings, this admonition stopped us in our tracks. Whatever did he mean, we wondered, when he uttered that last commandment: "Never worry how it looks." How could we not worry? Wasn't that the point, to worry about whether or not we were creating beauty? Now, after many years at the easel, I can explain it to you.

When Norman said "how it looks," he was thinking about how it looks to other people and the judgments they might make. We know that judgments on beauty are subjective, often based on cultural norms, and are certainly not conclusive in any way. How it looks is not a measure of beauty, or accomplishment, or anything important.

Fashions fade, standards are constantly morphing, what people declare is beautiful or ugly is not quantifiable or meritorious. What is relevant is whether the artist or author spoke from the heart, and with love, determination, and passion, brought all he knew and could concoct into the moment of creation. If he did that, spoke that truth, he made beauty, pure and simple, no matter how it looks.

In a three-hour model session in which I may do twenty or so drawings and sketches, probably only one or two survive the trash can. Why do I save the few efforts I find worthy? Because I see in them something true. Now what do I mean by true? I mean that I captured something, anything really—the feeling of the light, the weight of the pose, the model's extreme discomfort, something revealed about her character or her individuality.

Let me explain what I find compelling about it. Sometimes when a model is a no-show, we take turns drawing each other. This piece is a drawing of a fellow artist who sat for ten minutes or so, and I made a quick watercolor. I captured her quirkiness, her ageless adorableness. She made very quirky drawings herself, and when I look at this drawing, her personality floods back into my memory. I don't remember her name, but everything else I liked about her is here.

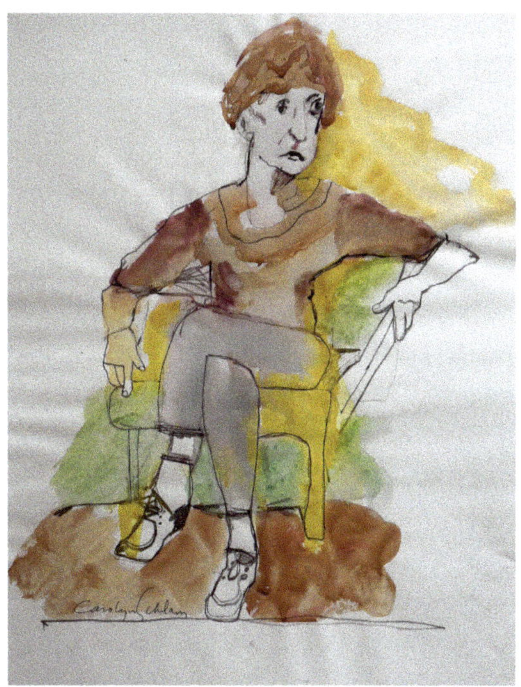

The Art Class, 2008, Ink, 24 x 18 inches

Each work has something to offer, something it excels at. In one, I like the way the figure fills the page with nothing extraneous. In another, there is a sculptural quality I like. Then maybe another shows a reasonable encapsulation of bone and flesh, and you can even guess where the model felt pain while holding that pose for twenty minutes. A work may have a graphic quality that makes the drawing punchy and animated, or a freshness or tenderness that enchants. Many forces are at work to set the artist's course and focus: the way the model presents, the mood of the day, maybe just how the first stroke or line makes a particular direction inevitable.

One of the distinguishing features of a good or beautiful work of art is that it is something you wish to look at. One might say, "the work is kind to the eye." There is something in it that holds your interest and invites you to keep looking.

Likewise, if the work displeases, I daresay there is something there that does not ring true. It may seem artificial and it "hurts your eyes." The color may be too bright. Something offends and you instinctively turn away.

I am not speaking here of the subject matter, rather the qualities of the work. Picasso's *Guernica* is a powerful statement of the horrors of war, and yet it is fascinating to look at. The same goes for many other works depicting gruesome scenes.

I am a great fan of wit and humor. I admire a complex puzzle or conundrum. I also admire irreverence, especially when it is done to turn a moldy old concept on its head. When I see true originality in art, I am delighted, and I can be as happy with a frivolous work as a weighty one. Expressiveness has so many components; some of them are freshness, personality, intimacy, vulnerability, directness, vigor, conviction, and humor. All of these, in my opinion, are qualities descended from and intertwined with love, and I will go into them in further depth in the next chapter.

I think it is very important, both for a working artist in any medium and for a viewer or lover of all the arts, to not only enjoy and savor, but to ask oneself what it is about a work that is compelling. We can't always put our finger on it. We say it is beautiful, or moving, or boring. But why, exactly? Finding out not only takes our enjoyment of the arts to the next level, it shows us something about ourselves.

Since I always advise others that we be as open as possible in life and in art, I love the big tent that expressiveness provides as criteria for understanding creative work. It provides the greatest protection against bigotry and the greatest possibility for each of us to live and work as the unique beings that we are.

Before I leave this subject, a little caveat, if you will permit me. I recently stopped in to see a museum exhibition with the interesting title *Defining Beauty*. The curators had selected the work of three artists whom they felt addressed this concept in a compelling way. As a viewer, I was interested in the qualities that these works possessed that made them beautiful—at least in the curators' view.

The museum's notes on beauty referred to the familiar saying, "Beauty is in the eye of the beholder," which reinforces that beauty is indeed subjective and not a fixed or even definable quality.

Clearly, no other curator seeking work emblematic of or "defining" beauty would have selected these same works, there being no criteria by which to mark any work as more beautiful than any other. It is a conundrum, to be sure. Is there anything we can all agree is beautiful?

As for this particular exhibition and the choices made, though I would not have selected these works, I applauded all of them as I universally champion every artist's effort to produce expressive, even beautiful work. The curators obviously found something in these works that superseded all the other works they rejected. Just like I asserted that one artist's view of a landscape says more about him than the landscape, I would suggest that the curators' choices said more about them than about the artists selected.

I can't help but think of the Yiddish saying *Mann Tracht, Un Gott Lacht* ("Man Plans and God Laughs"). What are we doing all this arguing for? Does it matter what each of us thinks is beautiful? So we disagree, so what?

Should we say "the more the merrier" and throw the arguments into the dustbin? Beauty, expressiveness—these are moving targets, and in the end, they just get us thinking, feeling, making distinctions, enjoying art, being alive, and of course, debating with others until we are, hopefully, finally laughing along with God.

Could that be just another way to describe enlightenment?

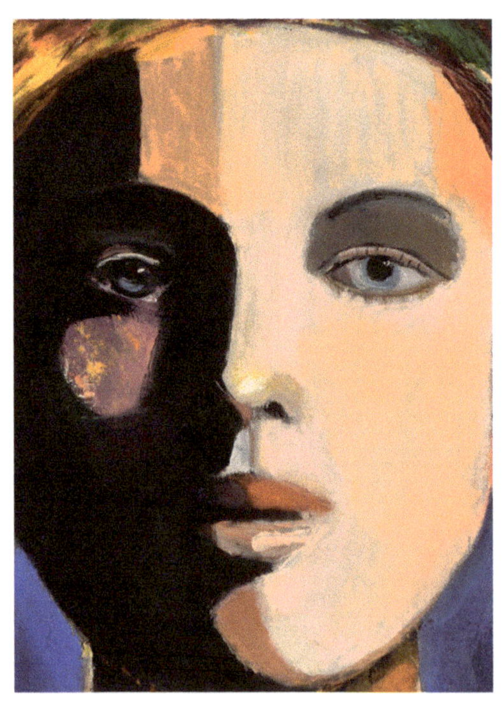

Blue, Oil on canvas, 30 x 24 inches

TEN

Love

"One's not half of two; two are halves of one."
—E. E. Cummings

Love, ah, the topic of topics. I saved it for last. I believe it underlies everything else we have discussed in this volume.

Love is a prerequisite for a good life. It is as essential to functioning for warm-bodied creatures as air and water. (It's possible that plants need a little love too.) If an animal or child fails to receive the loving care of its parent or other adult as a baby, its ability to grow well, learn, and develop to its full potential is severely compromised. We all know that.

Love is the greatest motivator. The urge to connect with the object of one's love, be it a person, an idea, or an activity, commands us to do our very best, to invent, create, demonstrate, be and do whatever will bring us closest to that aspiration.

Love is the most powerful emotion. It is the lion of the emotional jungle. All the other emotions hide in the bushes when love comes around; they don't stand a chance.

Love makes time irrelevant. Even a moment shared with a loved one coats the heart with joy. Just a little is a lot. One kiss takes us through a hard day and a long night.

Love is the greatest challenge the ego may ever face. It's the only thing that will make you choose another over yourself, risk your very existence with intention.

Love is a blessing. It is like a soft coat that wraps you in bliss, eliminating the cold and letting you walk blithely through the night, gazing at the stars.

Love is a guide. It keeps your step sure, your path lit, your destination in sight.

Love is the horizon. We all need that line that divides the now from the possible. We live in what we can see, but our dreams percolate and enliven our now. What is on the other side is the wonder. We need wonder in order to create.

Love is rapture.

Love is joy.

Love is what we live for and what we remember when we die.

Love is the meaning of life, the end all and be all of existence.

Love is all.

But this is not a romance book. It is a book about art, I remind myself. So, I posit, what does love have to do with making and appreciating art? Three words come to mind: purpose, kindness, and gratitude. Let's look at how they each manifest in art.

Purpose

Purpose is "the reason for which something is done or created or for which something exists." We might also use the word "intention." So I guess we should start by asking: What is the purpose of art?

We are born knowing nothing. Our bodies function automatically, and we are helpless. We depend on the love of others to survive. For a while we are unwritten. Do we even have a self? We are all possibility at this nascent stage.

Little by little we come into consciousness. We learn a few words, identify people and objects. We animate, become ambulatory, begin to explore. We learn our name, and we look up when we are called. We answer. Eventually, we become a conscious soul, a unique individual, and our possibilities, little by little, become enabled. We have thoughts, ideas, a personality, idiosyncrasies, and desires.

I don't mean to be matter of fact about this truly incredible evolutionary process that makes us who we are. The truth is that we do not start at zero and acquire traits and abilities. All of these are built in, already present, waiting. They enter the world like bulbs planted in the ground to suddenly bloom as conditions permit and the signal is given that it is time.

The person that we become is more than the accretion of all these traits. You cannot add them up and arrive at the sum that is you. Each trait and skill and propensity modifies the others, so the formula for you is truly unique, one of a kind. "A singular sensation," as they sang in *Chorus Line*. I always loved that song.

Each of us find many ways to communicate who we are through our activities and speech. But something propels some of us to invest ourselves in not only speaking but expressing ourselves through art. Why?

We say art is a calling, a strong urge to follow a particular path. For some the best way to share their feelings and thoughts is to convert them into art. I believe it's a calling of love, but love of what exactly?

Firstly, the artist must believe that her thoughts and feelings are good and worthy of being shared as they might benefit or entertain or enlighten another person. This is not a contradiction of loving. We nourish and love ourselves so we have something to offer.

Then there is love of the practice itself, the process of converting those thoughts and feelings into notes of music, poetry or prose, pixels of paint, chunks of wood, or marble. The artist will spend his life engaged in that process; he had better love the work because the material gain is iffy at best.

This desire to put oneself out there in an artistic format has to supersede the fear of rejection, and that's no small feat. Not everyone will like what we do, and the right to criticize and judge artistic effort is not only permitted in our society but encouraged. We've got to believe in ourselves to do the work and share it.

Lastly, there is love of and respect for the art form itself, which helps us see that art has value, brings joy to others, and is something the artist finds worthy of a lifetime of devotion.

These three targets for love are the guiding lights for artistic practice. They may ebb and flow at different rates through the artist's career, but without them, there is not the heart to do such difficult work. If only one of these loves falters, the artist may say that she is blocked, for it takes the free flow of all to commit to full and free expression.

If the artist doubts the art form or does not feel competent to express herself in it, if she doesn't believe in it or in herself, energy slumps and conviction is weak. This leads to shortcuts or half efforts, and that won't cut it. If the love is fierce, it sharpens the eye and enlivens the fingers, and magnificent artwork is possible.

The artist must believe in the merit of his subject. He is delivering a message with the work, and if he doesn't believe in it, the viewer probably won't either. A strong intention is key. My teacher, Norman Raeben, liked to have his students paint dirty and smelly things, like fish. He would cajole us to "put some dirt in the paint," and "put the smell in the fish." Now, how in the world do you accomplish that? we wondered, but having that strong intention intensified our practice.

How in the world do you paint a smell? This requires abstract thinking and a sensitivity that people not engaged in the arts may not develop. Since the artist must have enhanced sensitivity to create art, challenging oneself with these types of assignments is necessary. Consider the following:

- How do you express gravity?
- What is the color of water?

- How does bliss change a human face?
- What abstract shapes do I make to convey corruption?
- How can I express jazz music with paint?
- What does an angel look like?

These are questions non-artists may find silly, but to us, they are as basic as how to fix a leak, write computer code, or treat a burn. Dealing with these impossible questions is how we make our art.

The artist must not only express well; she must possess the skills and knowledge to make full use of her medium, and she must, most importantly, have something to say. The most exquisite talent will have no meaning if it fails to express something that is valuable, interesting, and needing to be said.

This brings us once again to purpose, for purpose is the engine that empowers the vehicle to take us somewhere wonderful.

On the next page is a painting I made to try to discuss a difficult subject—sexual abuse. You see a nude woman lying on the floor. She is painted with vivid pastel shades. In the background is a doorway in which you see only the shoes of a man. The shoes are black and they convey an ominousness to the painterly image of the woman. The composition asks: is he about to enter or has he left and is glancing back. Here the use of color and composition convey the emotion of the piece. The title is only one word—*Shoes*—because if the work is successful, it should speak without explanation.

Works like *Shoes* may be painful to look at. They are surely not decorative fanciful pieces that one would choose to hang over a couch or on a bedroom wall. I am reminded of the work of artist Anselm Kiefer whose canvases allude to the horror of the Holocaust. These types of works belong on the walls of museums where we may visit them and leave them behind. They are haunting. Think about the artist creating such an image and feeling the purpose to do so.

When an artist is working from a strong intention, the work has added meaning and consequence, and this encourages the artist to do his very best. Purpose engenders conviction, and conviction leads to an intensity in the effort that, hopefully, is transmitted to the viewer. As an artist becomes more confidant in her craft, the work can become more personal and therefore more purposeful.

Without purpose, the artist may wander, may be inclined to imitate either others or his former self. We all arrive at a point in our careers when we doubt ourselves, are tired of our own work, and feel empty. When this happens, the best thing is to move away from the easel and do something new, or perhaps just rest, waiting for renewed energy to point the way to a yet unsourced inspiration. As we rest or take a new road, a new intention can take shape.

Kindness

Singer and songwriter Randy Newman wrote a poignant song about human kindness titled "I think it's going to rain today"; I am hearing it in my mind's ear as I write this section. Kindness is a kind of reverence, a deep expression of love. It is powerful and energetic. It invigorates the universe. We all appreciate human kindness.

Note that love is not an emotion shared only between humans. It is a kind of reverence for life, an inner sun that extends its rays to everything outside, without privilege. So you can feel warmth toward an animal, a plant, a tree, a flower, a book, a paper, a brush, a tube of paint, anything and everything.

I live in a very lovely neighborhood with beautiful scenery, flowering plants, and since it is close to the mountains, many

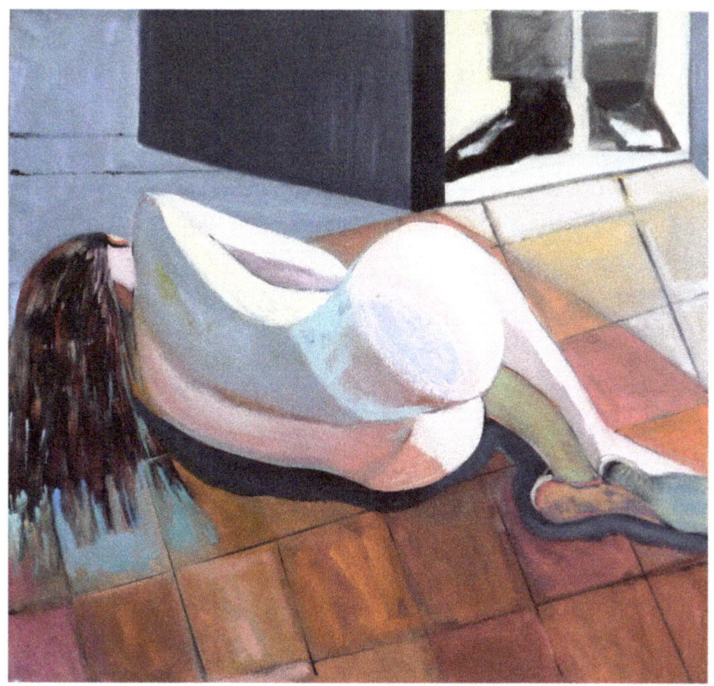

Shoes, 2016, Oil on canvas, 30 x 40 inches

residents other than humans: birds of all kinds, small animals like squirrels and bunnies, and many deer that come down from the hills to dine on our flowers. What a treat it is to take the dog out for an early morning walk and encounter some of these lovely creatures. All of us in the neighborhood talk about it and are excited to share our sightings. We have lovely weather too, and people enjoy strolling at all times of the day and night.

When we cross each other's paths, whether we are acquainted or not, it is the custom to wave, say hello, acknowledge the other's existence. People passing by in cars also wave and smile as a matter of course.

All this camaraderie has a terrific effect on me and, I suspect, on many others. It gives me the feeling that I belong, that I am part of this community. When people wave and say hello, and I do the same, we are telling the other that we acknowledge them, recognize their right to be in this place, and wish them well. You probably feel a similar connection in your own affinity group:

those you work with, fellow exercisers at the gym, dog walkers, musical theater patrons. We feel this type of connection on holidays with fellow shoppers before Thanksgiving, with people in the park. This is just regular, plain variety human kindness; but it is important, and it makes other things happen. That's why I call it energetic. What exactly do I mean?

When people wave and I feel recognized, my self-esteem gets a little boost. It puts a lilt in my step. Because I feel good, I am inclined to be thoughtful and helpful to others. The good feelings carry me through the day and seep into my work. My general good mood makes me more attentive and introduces a lightness that I apply to my tasks. I give my dog an extra treat.

We can probably all agree that this good will and cheerfulness is a boon to our lives and part of community building. But what bearing does it have on our discussion about art?

What does it mean to be kind to your artwork? Well, to be kind is to take care, to be consciously respectful. Though my "partner" may be inanimate, I extend my good will to all aspects of my task. So I make sure my canvas is stretched well and is nice and tight. I lay out a generous amount of paint—stinginess is not welcome here. I open the window and let in the fresh air. I take a deep breath as I step up to the easel. I apply the paint *con brio*—lovingly, with "spirit and enthusiasm."

Why? Because I care. And because I care, my painting gives back to me the love I am giving it, just like the people I am kind to who treat me likewise. The colors in my painting shine because I put them on so well. The drawing is strong because I did not hesitate.

The Buddhists refer to this as *karma*, meaning "action." The idea is that we create our perceptions and therefore our lives by what we do and how we conduct ourselves. You've heard the phrase: what goes around, comes around. I'm not sure who was the first to coin it, but no matter, the idea is that we have the power to act and our actions determine our path.

A small action can lead to a world of change, to amazing and unforeseen opportunities and consequences. Many people think of this as the universe cooperating with us. If the universe is the sum of all those lovely people waving and saying good morning, so be it.

Give this a whirl: Spread your human kindness like soft unsalted butter on a delicious bagel. It is guaranteed to make you smile and will make everything you do that day and every following day more enjoyable, peaceful, and gratifying. Spread good energy, and you will be doing your part to change the world. Think what would happen if everyone did the same. Kindness is not milk toast; it is a powerful energy-boosting, change-engendering action that can have marvelous repercussions in your life and the lives of others.

It can also have a huge effect on your art practice. Perhaps you never thought of applying the concept of kindness to your own work, but why not? Have you ever heard cooks attribute the secret ingredient in their dishes to be love? Likewise, the addition of kindness into your art practice can make your pixels of paint even more appetizing, your words chewier and crunchier, all of your efforts just more delicious.

Someone once paid me the greatest compliment, and I happily share it with you. She said, "You are a bright light. Keep shining." Isn't that what we all want to be? Practice kindness, and you are there!

Gratitude

We all have many losses and disappointments in life. There's no denying this or making believe it's not true. Though I am very positive, I am not a Pollyanna. I know life is hard.

Many years ago, I suffered a painful loss. Someone I had lived with for many years decided he no longer wanted me in his life, and I found myself surprisingly and painfully alone. I cried and cried and felt utterly lost.

Then one day a friend called and invited me to go with her

to a church service that Sunday. I am Jewish and so was she, so I was surprised at the ask, but happy to have somewhere to go, so I agreed.

She took me to a Unity church. I knew nothing about this group but later found this to be a nondenominational church that is quite inclusive and welcomes people of all faiths.

The service utterly astounded me. The gospel music pierced my heart, and I was mesmerized by the speaker, an older man with long white hair who delivered the most life-affirming message I had ever heard. I found myself crying throughout the service, to the surprise of my friend. I was so moved.

The following week and every week after for the next several years, I went to that church alone. My friend never came back. Her job, I now assume, was to deposit me there, her purpose satisfied after that first visit. Most of the services made me cry. I now realize that they opened me, and I was able to work out my feelings of loss.

The crying lasted about a year, but after the crying and the release of my pain, I went to church for the lessons, the messages delivered by the regular minister and all of the guest ministers. When I described where I was going to friends who could not fathom my regular church attendance, I called it the "love church" because that was what that church was to me—a place where love was celebrated. It was not the love of God or Christ because the church did not explain God as a being or entity. It was what they called the "Christ consciousness," and it does not reside in any one figure. We all have it. We are all part of the love that is divine.

The message overall was that to obtain whatever you want in your life, you must become it. To find love, be loving. To find truth, be truthful. To find peace, be peaceful. The minister used the word "abundance" a lot. He explained that you could see the world in one of two ways: as a place with limited resources, a place of scarcity; or a place of abundance. If you believe the former, that beauty and love and all things good are in limited supply, you would have to compete with others to receive your fair share. If, on the other hand, you believe that there is enough to go around, there is no need to compete. We can all share, and we would all have enough. The first route leads to fear, competition, struggle, and potential harm. The second leads to harmony, love, and fulfillment. An easy choice, if you ask me.

To practice abundance thinking, what does one need to do? Well, obviously you need to be open-minded, respectful to all, loving, and able to recognize all fellow humans as equally worthy. Above all, the message was to be grateful.

This kind of thinking was referred to as "new age wisdom," but it is very close to the lessons of the Zen masters, the path so similar to the Eightfold Path of the Buddhists. This kind of thinking is integral to the concept of *dharma* ("right action"). Really, is there any difference? Isn't this understanding of abundance on the same trail as the path to enlightenment?

I believe I received a *satori* or moment of enlightenment when I realized the true meaning of abundance. To realize that everything is available for our good and that we can accept it as our rightful inheritance is to receive the liberating knowledge that we are entitled to be happy. This is a reason to rejoice! All we need do to claim this inheritance is to be grateful.

I learned to be grateful, and it changed my life; it didn't just heal the pain I felt, but it turned everything upside down and inside out. Made me a better, kinder, more thoughtful person. Made me Carolyn, the Carolyn I was born to be.

So before you criticize, belittle, downplay, mock, mistreat yourself or anyone else, practice gratitude. It has a way of neutralizing even real and deep pains and distresses.

When your knee hurts, be grateful that your stomach is fine and you can look forward to a good meal. When someone has not reached out to you, be grateful you can make the call. When you mess up the painting you had some hopes for, be grateful you learned what constituted the mess. You won't be going there again.

Being grateful always affirms the good that is always present. It is healing to speak words of gratitude to yourself and others. Watch someone's face closely when you tell them how much they mean to you. The lines of the face relax, and a smile is born. Watch them receive that love in a simple sentence: *I am so glad you are my friend*, or *What would I do without you?*

Sharing feelings of gratitude is the act of giving praise to others. It is truly the best gift and the one most remembered. Just like I have applied the concept of kindness to artmaking, we can likewise do the same for gratitude.

I am so grateful that I have had the opportunity in this life to make art. Yes, I have chosen this path, but I have been supported by others in so many ways. I got to be born at a time and place where it was possible for a female to do this work, where my basic needs were provided for, giving me the space to dream. So many others do not have this choice.

So how can I apply this deep gratitude in my practice? I can remind myself that I am blessed to have this time to make art, and I can take the time to do it well. That consciousness of my good fortune will be manifest in the seriousness and devotion I apply to my task. I will also be mindful that it might not have been this way and endeavor to remain humble about my gift. I believe that will help me to not over-promise or aggrandize what I have accomplished. This will just take me to the next day when I can hope to do even better.

There isn't anything you can do that is more powerful than to be grateful. Gratitude is an offering from one heart to another. It is a yes to the universe, to life, to love. Give it to yourself, and before long you'll be showering the flowers with it, kissing dogs and strangers, and learning, as I did, that gratitude is your ticket to happiness and fulfillment, no matter how your story goes.

Love, Yes Please

Before I close on the subject of love (impossible) and move on to our last chapter dedicated to experimentation in art, I want to put love in the context of what we have discussed in previous chapters. Let's connect the dots.

In our first chapter—"Awakening"—we talked about inspiration. The initiation. Finding and then savoring the opening of our creativity. The green light to go. The preparation of our perception and consciousness so we might be ready and able to create, to be.

What kind of being has an inspiration? That is such a monumental occurrence—to receive the impetus to do something, never mind something wonderful. One has to have consciousness to know it has been received. One must have energy and heart to do something with it. To begin.

The received must believe it is possible, and not only that, but the receiver must be capable and charged to oblige. That takes courage.

In order to love, one has to reach beyond oneself. The ego has to take a backseat. That is the meaning of compassion: identify with the other and feel what they are feeling. This is easy to understand when the object of our compassion is a living being. But we can and must learn compassion as artists. How can I show loving compassion for the object of my art?

Let's say I am painting a tree. My intention may be more specific; say I am drawing the tree in a storm. In my painting reverie, I actually identify with that tree, imagining the cold air that touches it, the gust that bends a branch, the lightning that threatens to sear it. I am enlivening my imagination with compassion, or in other words, I am making art with my feelings. This informs all my artistic choices. It brings tension to my arm as I draw the branch and gives me a felt line. It brings a quality to my color when I feel the cold air.

There is a tremendous difference one can discern between art that is descriptive and art that is felt. The latter has a vibrancy and tenderness that can only be achieved through loving attention. In Zen the word for this level of attention is *samadhi*, which is defined as "the highest state of mental concentration that people can achieve while still bound to the body and which unites them with the highest reality."

Samadhi is usually thought to be achieved through meditation, but as I have said, there are many ways to meditate, and artmaking can bring the artist into a meditative state. Truly inspired practice, loving practice, can deliver one to this state of realization through identification, immersion in, and worship of subject.

In our "Simplicity" chapter, we talked about clarity of mind, authenticity, and grace. Though love is not a much-discussed subject in Zen, the foundation of Zen is the realization of human suffering and how we can, through meditation and good acts, accept our human condition in its entirety, and rise to find joy. Christianity is much more direct in discussing love of the unconditional kind, which their exemplar Jesus embodied. Grace is a Christian concept that is a result of the unconditional love (*agape*) of God.

What does love have to do with simplicity? Once again, love of our medium and our message exhorts us to use it wisely, to not overdo so as to make the object of our love primary. Not to obfuscate or conceal, rather to service our love as best we can—simply, directly, and powerfully. It takes courage to speak simply, as the lack of ambiguity reveals the truth more purposefully. When we do not cloud or conceal our choices, they stand proudly, and nakedly, undeniably there. So simplicity is also an act of love; by choosing it we show our commitment to our art.

As we go about our lives and face an unknown future, having self-esteem emboldens us to see the world as a benevolent place, to imagine that we will be safe, that we can venture out and, good or bad, survive to live another day. The fact that we feel loved and respected gives us the courage to be bold; without it, we hold back, and this severely curtails our ability to be experimental, to improvise, to trust, and to try.

Reaching out and giving love challenges our creativity. It gives us a reason to move on and to accept change. To look for the beauty and good in what we encounter. It is fuel to move, and movement is life.

We've talked a lot here about perception and how it colors everything we do and feel. Perceiving the world with eyes of love truly affects how we feel about time, about the conditions we find ourselves in, our health, what is valuable, our self-esteem, how we present ourselves to the world, how we evaluate the things that happen to us.

I am very fond of the simple affirmation to "just walk on the sunny side of the street." It seems so obviously wise, and it is hard to believe that anyone could possibly disagree. What could the opposite recommendation be? "Be realistic." But why?

I could give you many other prescriptive "be's" that will take you a lot further. How about "Be happy" "Be kind" "Be grateful."

Love is at the root of positive thinking and right action. It is the impetus to do all the affirmative things we have discussed here, and without it, we are weakened, fearful, and reluctant.

Cultivating love is a practice as meaningful and necessary as meditation, and as essential to the human soul as any nourishment. Though the ability to love is inherent, as every baby looks to its mother with eyes of pure devotion, the struggles of everyday life erode this ability, requiring us to be active and conscientious stewards of love for ourselves, our families, communities, the natural world, and for our work.

We have talked about acceptance, joy, gratitude, purpose, clarity, perspective, grace, acceptance, authenticity, spontaneity, freedom, bliss—all the rewards of life, and they all are embedded and founded in love. All roads lead back to this one. Most songs are about this subject.

If we forget all words, but remember this one . . .

If we bear difficulty, and let this be our deliverance . . .

If we are sick and tired, but receive this gift . . .

We are okay. Our life has value. Our art lives on.

Zen and Buddhism do not linger on love in any of its forms, but love underlies the philosophy. Why follow the Eightfold Path if not for love? Why perform the regular practice of zazen if not for love? Why seek enlightenment at all? Only for the love of life and others who live.

Why make art if not for love? Contrary to popular assumptions, making art is not fun in the sense that riding a roller coaster may be described as such. Art is trying, messy, and difficult. Making art takes a huge effort. The results can disappoint. It's certainly not all rainbows and ice cream cakes.

We do it for the same reason we seek a lover. We seek a lover so we may share ourselves—all we know and all we are—with someone who will understand and appreciate us. Isn't that the underlying reason we make art? To experience our truth fully and joyfully and to share it with the world. To connect. Deeply and meaningfully. To appreciate and be appreciated.

Love goads us in our search for beauty, in our drive to express. After all, what is it that we want so desperately to express? The red glossiness of the skin of the apple? The incredible bond of a mother and child? The light as it dances over the ocean? These sensory realities enthrall and inspire us. We are not content just to see and admire them; we need to share the way they move us in a work of art. The urgency to do so is driven by their very evanescence, their miraculous, indescribable essence.

So underlying all that we do is this need to share. We may never see the people who admire our works. But in the making of them, we are reaching out, talking to them, putting our arms around them. Sharing our moments and our very existence. All for love, and love for all.

Thank you for reading my words and for allowing me to share some of my art. I assure you it was all created in love. Thank you for walking with me. May your days be filled with love, joy, gratitude, and if you are so inclined, art.

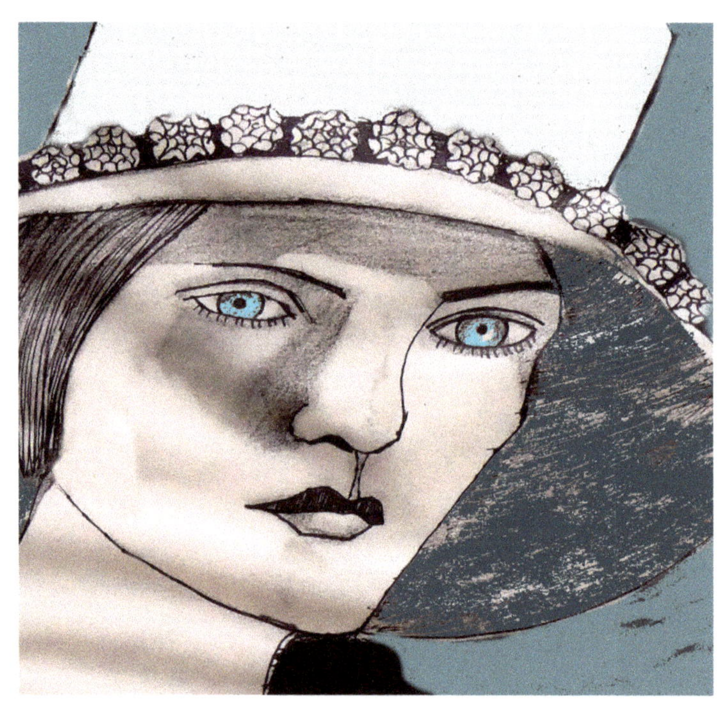

The Hat, Drawing, 24 x 18 inches

APPENDIX

Studio Diary

When you have been doing something for a long time, your tracks are often so deep you just can't get out of them. You keep repeating what has previously worked or not, as the case may be, following those old patterns. As an artist, you have spent countless hours standing at the easel, perhaps working from the same subject matter, using the same colors, making the same shapes, and it is all so tiresome. *I just want to do something new,* you tell yourself.

I am obviously talking about myself here, though many may identify. I am trying to be in the moment, but all my prior moments are bossing me around. What to do?

I have reached the end of this book, telling other people how great it is to live in the moment, to practice art in the Zen way. So, it's time for me to follow my own advice. I have decided to toss my tired habits to the curb and play! Yes, play.

I am going to do some things that are unfamiliar, that don't fit into the groove of my entrenched habits. I recommend this path to others: try an entirely new medium, a new subject, different tools, new prompts, sitting rather than standing (or vice versa), try anything that is not what you are used to doing.

I have worked in a variety of studios, drawing, painting and making collage for many years. As most of us probably do, I use many of the same structures and strictures I learned in art school. I use the same materials, even the same palette to place my paints on. It is pitted and distressed after decades of daily use. I usually put the colors in the same place so they are like the keys on a qwerty keyboard; I don't even have to look down to find them.

For many years, I have been a figurative artist, working from life, models, photographs, sketches, and developing imagery that is sometimes semi-abstract, sometimes impressionistic, sometimes more graphic, but pretty much representational, that is, a translation of something, if not highly detailed, still recognizable.

Of course, I have walked many roads to my destination, and one of the things I love about being an artist is that no two trips or days are the same. There is repetition certainly, but a detour always seems to present itself, and I often wind up in a place I never intended to go. That's truthfully the fun of it and the wonder of making art. You think you know what you're doing, but pretty much every day's practice includes a curve of some kind, an unintended bit of scenery that pops into view. One thing leads to another. We flit like bees from flower to flower, pollinating our art.

It all happens without interference or direction. Only now, for this book, I am throwing myself that curve. I am giving myself the assignment of making five abstract, nonrepresentational paintings. No models, no life studies, no photographs, no crib sheets, nada. Just blank canvases ready to receive whatever pictures might pop out of my brain.

I have not done this for a very long time. When I first left art school, I made some abstract paintings, fairly large ones, in fact. Before I started this experiment, I went to my warehouse and pulled them out. They had been taken off the stretchers as I never intended to show them. They had been rolled up for years, and the color was faded, the surfaces worn.

I studied them. They all would probably fly under the banner of lyrical abstraction. All focused on color relationships, and a feeling of deep space. You might see them as landscapes, though not representing any particular place, and strikingly, decidedly horizontal, lacking much in the way of anything vertical, like a tree or a building. Organic, floating shapes in space.

What would I do now, starting fresh? Truthfully, my mind was blank. But I had to start somewhere. Help!!!!

Wait a minute. I can do this, I tell myself.

An artist can start anywhere, with any word, any shape, any idea, and make something of it, relate it to something that matters to her and expresses something personal and maybe even universal. After all, people have an awful lot in common, live in the same world, and see the same sun rising every morning and retreating every night. So why wouldn't we share visions and imagery?

Sometimes I see my path as a game where all the roads lead to the same destination. Wherever I start, I wind up in that place. You have to think the reason is that, no matter how I try to paint like someone else, it is still me doing it. I can only wind up where only I was meant to go. The only place with my name on it. My town.

I remind myself that every work of art begins as abstract, even one that winds up being super realistic, even photographic. Picasso agreed, as he is purported to have said: "There is no abstract art. You must always start with something. Afterward you can remove all traces of reality." All I will be doing is taking a much longer ride on the abstract part of the trip and resisting the urge to make visual identifications. I vow to stay in the beautiful beginning, as I have urged here in my first chapter. Just stay there without end.

But I need a nail to hang my hat on, so I start by picking five words or concepts that I will consider in making these five pieces. After much thought, I select these: sensuality, play, innocence, wisdom, and light. I decide I will begin by creating a color ground on each canvas. Sensuality will be orange; play, yellow; innocence, pale green; wisdom, sky blue; and light, pale violet. I go to Home Depot and have the paint mixed. At this point, needless to say, I am very optimistic this will all work.

As I think about it now, after all that has happened, these color choices seem cliché, obvious. Had I realized this at the beginning, I would have scrapped this whole idea, but at the time, nothing else came to mind. Were my prior references—the models and still lives I worked from—a crutch? Something to rely on? Or perhaps they were my inspiration, just a branching off point. A turbo charge for my imagination. I guess I will find out, won't I? I forge ahead.

This is the nature of improvisation, which is what I am doing. I literally have no script and am walking cluelessly onto the stage. I will have to see what happens and where this all leads. I will have to trust my own reactions when they come and play along until my destination comes into view.

The thing to remember is that while I am the actor reacting to cues, I am also the author of this play. That means that I am a witness to the improvisation, and if it doesn't pass muster to my alter ego, the author, it will never get to the audience. Indeed, that is what may happen here.

This initial thinking led me to do some writing about color, which is my starting point on this experiment. Before I relate the rest of this story, I will share that writing. I think it is interesting in and of itself.

On Color

Who doesn't love color? It singularly dresses up the world. How dull would it be to live in black and white? We feel deprived if we know a film will be sans color, don't we?

We all love color but a painter not only enjoys it; she needs it like a bird needs a branch to rest on. The painter has an intimate connection with color. As a language with a rich vocabulary, it enables her imagination. She chooses her colors critically and applies them wisely. Without them, there is no message, no purpose, no sense.

I swim every day, and this usually sets my mind to wandering. Today, as I engineered my laps, the subject of color entered my mind. I opined that if I had to choose my favorite color, it would be aqua. Is it everybody's favorite? Perhaps not. What does aqua convey?

Water, of course, pops up first and foremost. Though we cannot name the color of water as it has no color of its own and just steals from the surrounding light, a greenish blue color that represents *agua* (aqua with a "g") comes first to mind. So what does it mean to me?

Aqua is purity. It washes away all impurities; they bow to its sovereignty. It is radiant. It is happiness and freedom. Yes, it is wonderful.

But now what of the other colors? I use them all and need them all. What is their purpose? I decide this is a worthwhile subject to add to this book as a feeling-thought, one that may ask you to consider your own propensities and what they mean to you.

Before I do, let me say that for a painter, color and texture are twins, and one has no power without the other. Just as important as the hue and value is the application. It can be transparent, translucent, thin and watery or drenched with oil, impacted and thick, gooey, dry, crusted, dusty, matte, glittering, glossy, and all these to infinitesimal degrees of variance.

And mixtures, let's not forget about that. There are so many nuances to play with. Painters are mixologists. A pinch of yellow, a soupcon of rose, a poke of cobalt blue changes everything.

Then the two no-colors—black and white—adding these to color mixtures has an immeasurable consequence. Why? White is light, and adding it tells volumes about placement, size, aerial perspective, and is absolutely crucial in creating a three dimensional illusion. Then there's black. Black turns color from a circus show into poetry. It is the voice of subtlety, as it softens and subdues color. Both black and white tell the story of atmosphere, and let's face it, atmosphere or air is what makes life on earth possible at all. In painting, they are our most essential additives.

OK, so back to our wondrous spectrum of color:

RED

The primary power color, there is nothing understated about red. It means business. It is passion, fire, love, boldness, and brilliance. It is, yes, BLOOD. Life incarnate. It is daring and fierce, and it doesn't equivocate. There's no ignoring it or letting it sit on the sidelines, is there? Red doesn't kid around.

ORANGE

It's not red, is it? It's friendlier, not so insistent. It's hot but it doesn't burn. It makes me think of things that grow, showy things, like flowers and fruits, which are gay and pleasing and delicious. Truly, you can't go wrong with it, but it doesn't dominate. It's not around that much. It punctuates, rather than soothes. But we're glad it's here as it jazzes up things in a kind of sweet way.

PINK

A minority voice, so to speak, but undeniable associations with femininity make its inclusion here essential. What shall we make of this connection? Let's see. Pink is sweet, it's soft, and it definitely does not offend—except perhaps in the hot variety which speaks with a bit more spunk. How do we like to imagine girls and women? As shades of pink? Baby pink, peachy pink, purplish pink, or the hothouse variety? So undeniably pretty, though our fondness cloaks shame.

YELLOW

Oh, yes, the sun, of course. Now this is a happy, happy color. After all, it is keeping us warm. There are two very distinct varieties though: the lemon hue is bright and bubbly while the mustard hue is a bit more aggressive, don't you think? It has a bite. The lemon can be sharp, but it isn't mean like the mustard variety, which kind of kicks ass, don't you think? Yellow has its moods.

GREEN

People think green is the easiest color on the eyes. It's in the middle of the spectrum, so that could be why. Also, it is the color of growing things, and we have to be fond of that. There are many, many greens, and each has a slightly different spin. It's not a primary color, and as a mixture of mighty blue and vivacious yellow, it can go in many directions. Let's face it, we could not live without it. It is wondrous and welcoming and wise. I adore it deeply, almost as much as blue.

BLUE

Color of colors, the third in the primary triad, and I see it as the big brother of its siblings, red and yellow. Blue is sky and heaven. It is goodness and strength. It knows who it is, confidant and loving. We look up to it and adore it. Always a first choice, a leader. It speaks with so many accents and voices. Beautiful BEATIFIC blue.

PURPLE

What happens when you take the divine blue and mix it with vivacious red? Oh, my! You get the most mysterious, temperamental color in the world. Purple. Oh there's mauve and alizarin and rose, and magenta, too, all the myriad shades. Purple, you are an enigma.

Color—so many manifestations, an endless array. Your expressive possibility is bountiful. You bless me and I am grateful. You awaken my imagination and catapult me to joy!

The Experiment

Back to the experiment. After I chose the base colors for my five artworks, I wrote down some of the associations I had for the subjects to possibly help guide me with shape making. Here are those associations:

For sensuality: curves, crevices, intensities, hard and soft

For innocence: veils, hidden spaces, washes of pale color, fantasy, trees, box, water

For wisdom: clarity, order, ladder, defined shapes

For play: upside down, circles, chaos, swing

For light: star, distance, faintness

Now, reviewing these, I see more cliches, more obvious choices. But I humor myself—you do not know until you know, right? And frankly, at this point, I don't know what I am in for. I move on.

Instead of focusing on my figurative work with its emphasis on the illusion, emotive content taking a back seat to believable renderings, my intention is to bring the expressive qualities front and center, eschewing all specific and identifiable references to actual objects.

I will begin with a color that will act as a foil or inspiration for the work. Since these works will be abstract, color and shape will be the main actors. My intention is to attempt to develop a new expressive vocabulary.

These five paintings will be abstract, nonobjective, but will they truly be nonrepresentational? These terms are used interchangeably to discuss art that is not descriptive. In abstract art, the images presented cannot be named. The familiar genres—landscape, figurative, still life—are all objective, though they can present in many ways: photographic, impressionistic, semi-abstract. It is objective because it refers to something that is identifiable, even if it is only suggested.

I ask myself: *If these abstract works do not represent anything, what are they about?*

I posit: *They might be color studies, geometric compositions, decorative surfaces, designs, and not refer to anything objective.*

But cannot the color studies have a temperature, suggest an environment? Cannot the geometric compositions resemble parts of objects? Is the decorative surface or design reminiscent of a culture, does it conjure a location or a time of day?

The question comes to mind: *If I translate a feeling, can someone say that I am representing it?*

This is more complex than I thought. My philosophical mind ratchets up. I see questions, problems, conundrums, and enigmas ahead.

I ask: *What do you call something that does not represent anything? Is it a NO-THING? NOTHING? Or is it more correct to say that what is represented is hidden or disguised?*

I ponder this: *How, in fact, do you make a no-thing? A not?*

Truthfully, this makes a knot in my brain.

The assignment: How to make a painting with no references.

Does that mean it doesn't say anything? THEN WHY MAKE IT AT ALL?

Or am I saying something so no one knows what it is? Is it a trick? Is the message of the abstract painting a secret? Is the message that there is no message? As the speaker, how can I not say something or rather, say something that no one understands? Is this a double negative?

This makes me think of the politicians in office who do not believe in government. *What are they there for? And what am I, the painter, here for?* I am confused.

In my heart I want to do the opposite of what this assignment encourages, not only say something but say it emphatically, represent loudly and proudly. How in the world can I do this?

Possibly the best way to think about this is to relate it to the idea of show and tell. It is a commonly agreed-upon concept that good fiction does not tell; it shows. This means that the message the author wants to convey is not concretely told in the text. It is suggested, or shown, alluded to, or intended to be discerned from the way the characters behave and speak.

Can I apply this concept to image making? To abstract painting?

What if I analogize that the colors and shapes play the part of the characters, and the way they behave suggests and conveys a mood or an emotion that must be extracted by the viewer. It has not been presented, or told, by the artist.

Nonetheless, bemused and somewhat worried, I begin. I'm hoping I will figure it out as I go.

Abstract Painting #1

My initial intention is to create something one could describe as sensual or as suggesting the characteristics of sensuality. Sensuality is not a thing; it is a quality.

If my subject is sensuality, which is a quality, can one consider this a representation? I am obviously NOT representing an object, but I clearly do have an objective.

Object vs. Objective. Is this only semantics?

I apply the orange as my tone. This choice means that I am saying sensuality is "represented" by a warm shade since we associate warmth with pleasure and pleasure with sensuality.

I proceed. *What to paint?* I am stumped.

I am so accustomed to connecting my color and shape choices to a subject that the lack of subject is rendering me mute. This is really difficult.

I begin to apply paint to the canvas, choosing what I determine to be luscious colors in interesting relation to one another.

I make a circle in the upper right. Immediately I see it as a sun. OOPS. Representation.

I try to disguise it.

In the lower half, I apply some burnt sienna. This is a very transparent paint, and I take a rag and soak it in linseed oil and then rub the burnt sienna into whorls. I love the way it goes on and the way it looks. It resembles oiled wood. OOPS. Representation.

But I remind myself that the whorls don't assume a recognizable shape that you can name. I leave them. I break them up with some grayish green, a color I love. It is a wonderful partner to the woody quality I have introduced.

Who's kidding whom? The painting is beginning to look like a landscape, only the good news is that it is not a specific place I have studied and painted. It is imaginary. It is a composite of something that feels like sky and something that feels like wood. I leave the sun; a circle can be anything, can't it? And it's a legitimate geometric shape.

I don't know at this point if the painting makes any sense or that it even has to make sense. Once again, if there is no representation, does logic or sense even apply?

I have always believed that works of visual art do have a kind of internal logic and that the creator is guided by this logic, knowing intuitively when a note is discordant and must be changed or eliminated. Frankly, in spite of this belief, I am really not sure whether this painting violates those principles and is actually a pastiche. In trying to avoid representation, am I making something devoid of sense or meaning?

Truthfully, I cannot answer my own questions. I do not know what I have done. In spite of this, at some point I have to determine that I am finished with this particular effort, that adding another note or changing what I have already done is ill-advised. I stop and subsequently decide that I will call the painting *Sienna*.

This makes me think that abstract artists giving so-called nonrepresentational paintings a name seems to obviate or call into question the premise for this genre. How can you name something that is unnameable, and if you do, isn't it a cheat? Isn't it representational after all, but just represents something more evanescent or sophisticated or complex than an object? A

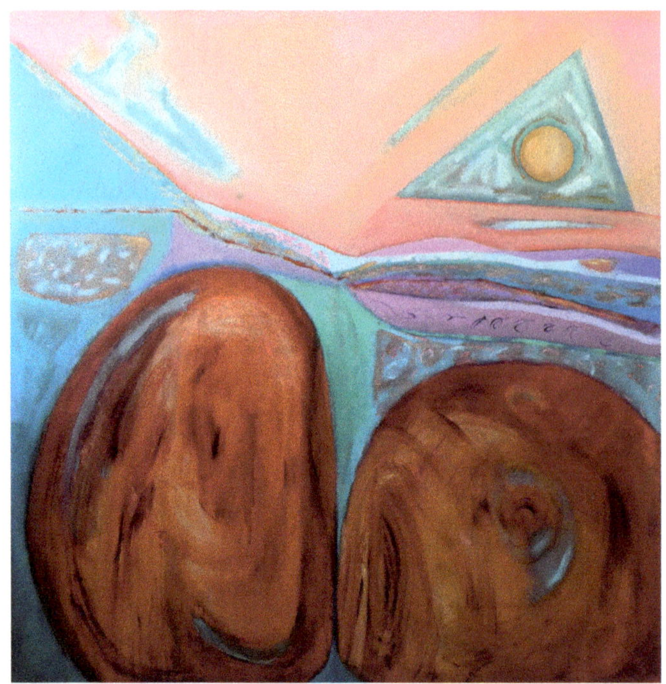

Sienna, 2022, Oil on canvas, 48 x 48 inches

feeling? If a painting can represent a feeling, a mood, a quality, a concept, a word, can't we say that it is, in fact, representational? It is likewise objective, as there is an object in mind, seemingly encapsulated in the artwork, be it in disguised form.

If artists and art historians are saying that abstract art does not represent a bonafide object like a chair, apple, face—a noun—but instead something more complex, well, so what? This does seem to take the gravitas or virtue out of abstract art "for its own sake."

I am not convinced that making abstract art is something that interests me, but I have committed to making these five works. Perhaps I will learn something important that may light the way for future endeavors.

I decide that I will allow *Sienna* to rest and return to it after I have completed the other four pieces. I have junked the concept of sensuality, but it indeed was the genesis for this painting, now named for the whorls that I created.

Returning to the visual ideas I had assigned to this piece—

curves, crevices, intensities, hard and soft—are they present? Yes, but the follow-up question is: What have I accomplished here? Have I shown sensuality without describing or telling it?

Abstract Painting #2

After completing *Sienna*—or just putting it aside for now—I am dubious about continuing to interpret these five concepts. I consider doing the Innocence piece, but for the life of me, I cannot conjure anything. I decide to drop the idea, at least for this next piece, and just paint, improvise, lay paint onto canvas and see what percolates.

Many painters work this way. Instead of starting with a concept or intention, we just paint *al primo*, without plan, letting the paint tell us where to go. It is an associative, instinctual, improvisational way to work, and I decide to just follow this path and see what turns up.

Once again I come up with a bath of blue and streaks of color. This seems to be all I am capable of. I see that this second piece also resembles landscape. It is, shall we say, landscape-light or landscape-like. True to my cliché mind, whenever I see streaks or bodies of blue, I invariably think of water. I introduce lots of other colors, but the blues predominate.

I've mentioned it in this book but it's worth talking about again in this context. One of the things that blocks creativity is the affection that develops for what one has already done. This is happening here. Though I have recognized this work as landscape-light, I have to admit that I admire these streaks of color living in the blue and am loathe to change them. I have become attached.

This happens in artmaking, as in life, and when it does, we often find that we have settled for something just okay when moving on might have brought us something even better. Sometimes the affection is not strong enough to keep me from forging on bravely to that unknown territory, but today that is

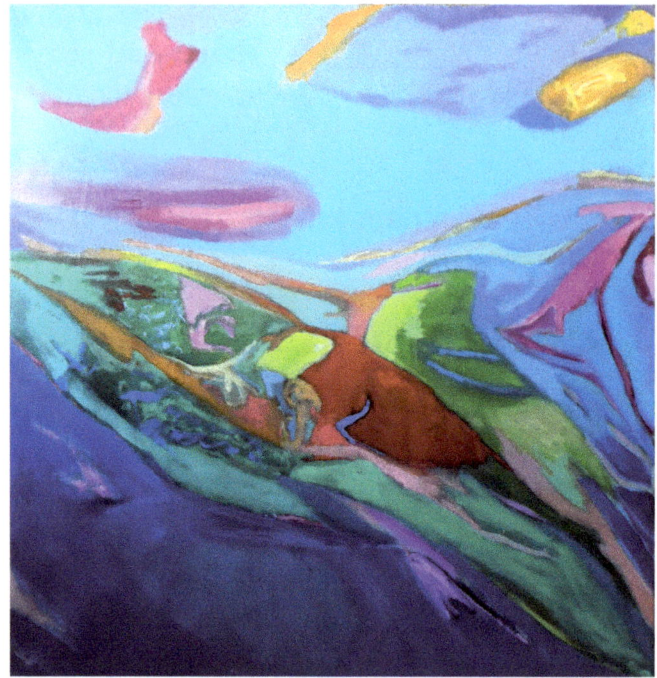

Beyond the Blue, 2022, Oil on canvas, 48 x 48 inches

not the case. I decide I like the blue world just a little too much to destroy it or even change it.

I decide I will call the painting *Beyond the Blue*.

Titles for visual art are usually afterthoughts and often are about associations. This is especially the case when the work evolves on the canvas without a preset script. That is the case here.

This may be a trite title, but it has particular significance for me. My dear mother, who has been gone from this earth over thirty years, had a few songs she loved and sang repeatedly to me and my two sisters. One of these was "Beyond the Blue Horizon," and I always loved that song, both the melody and the words, which include: "Beyond the blue horizon, lies a beautiful light . . . Goodbye to fears that haunt me, joy is waiting for me." Thinking about that song floods back memories of my mother's lovely face with her radiant smile, singing to "her girls." As one of those girls, the notes rained down on me and made me smile, and I smile today when I remember the love she shared.

This association makes me even less likely to make changes to this work. Now that I have linked it to my mother, every note, every shade of color seems that much more significant.

Of course, the viewer seeing this work, and even learning the title, will have no idea of my associations, but isn't this the case with most artworks we view? We judge the work on how it appears. There is no way to read my relationship with my mother by looking at *Beyond the Blue*. I have to hope that my feelings found their way into my fingertips, to the colors I mixed, and onto the canvas. Whether you can read the careful choices as love, I cannot know. I let it be, and move on to my next effort.

Abstract Painting #3

Abstract #2 made me think of my mother's songs, and so for #3 I decide I will try to depict another of her favorites. Based on my experience making the sensuality piece, I have decided these words, concepts, are just too precious for this experiment, and also, that I apparently do not have the imagination to transfer them to imagery. Perhaps subjects that have more emotional pull will make visualization possible.

Lately I have taken to playing the piano. I played as a child, mostly classical music, but now I do it just for my own pleasure. I usually play around dinnertime while dinner is on the stove, and though I have a few books of classical music, my very favorites are jazz standards and Broadway musicals. I love the melodies and lyrics of these old songs, and sometimes I sing along as I play.

Mom was very sentimental, and she loved the musical *The Man of La Mancha*. The lead song in that show is "The Impossible Dream," which is in my repertoire. Whenever I play that emotional, even schmaltzy song, I think of my mother who loved it so much. The song is about reaching for the stars—the

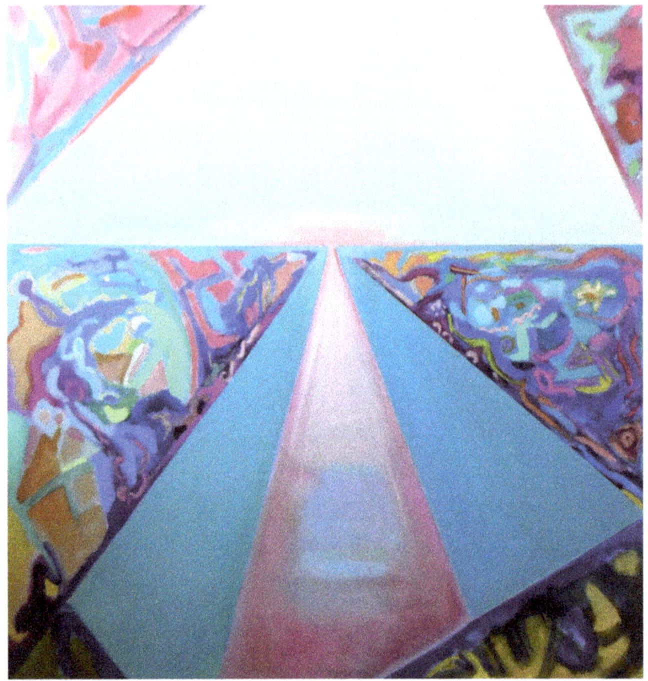

The Impossible Dream, 2022, Oil on canvas, 48 x 48 inches

unreachable stars—and that was what my mother wanted for her children. She died before she had a chance to see my artwork or read my books, but when I play this song on the piano, I feel I am telling her I have aimed for those stars.

So why not? I decide I will paint "The Impossible Dream." Hopefully, emotion will guide my way.

But, really, how do you depict reaching for a dream?

My cliché factory starts churning. I don't want to do something as literal as a hand reaching out into space; that would immediately take me out of the nonobjective mode. But my prosaic mind can't seem to come up with anything other than another imaginary place where the dream is way out in the distance.

I don't want to identify what the dream might be, just the placement, but with an energy drawing the eye to that place. I am painting a pathway. Because the dream is impossible, I decide not to use naturalistic colors. After all, this is a fantasy. I do know that I want the colors to be fresh and lively. There will be no mud in my impossible dream, nothing tarnishing the sheer positivity of it or giving it any sense of reality. This dream is impossible, after all.

I mock up the design, but have a problem with how to show the faraway place where the dream lives. I first think of it as a doorway, or an archway, which I draw first. But then when I look at it, it seems to resemble a tombstone, and I don't want my dream painting to convey death, so I scrap that. I next settle on just a doorway that is a rectangle, but that doesn't work either.

In the end, I settle on just the light—a blazing light in the distance where the dream can live—and the long road that goes there. It may be an obvious or well-worn idea, but it is one that I share. In fact, the long road—our life—is itself the dream.

Whether we reach the goal is almost an afterthought. In truth, as we walk on, the dream expands. It will always be impossible. Nonetheless, in the reaching, there is the now of the path. This is the unspoken text of this painting.

The iteration may be trite, but the idea is worthy. When I look at the painting, I find something lovely there. Is it possible that what may be trite in one medium may be radiant in another? Though I took my inspiration from a set of words, the painting now stands on its own, speaking in its own language. I am thinking my mother might approve.

Abstract Painting #4

Of all the original themes, the one I was most anxious to work on was play. I was thinking of primary colors and exuberant shapes. I chose a bright yellow, and my goal was to suggest the frivolity of play without defining any particular games or devices or players. I thought it would be a lot easier than it turned out to be.

My images of play were too concrete. I imagined swings, bubbles, various things upside down, and the like. If I were Paul

Klee, one of the most playful painters, this would be second nature. Everything he did gave off a playful persona, as if all of his constructions were actually made from legos and tinker toys instead of beautifully applied paint and delicate lines.

But for me, not so much. I make shapes that look like swings and slides, which is too cliché even for me. In the end, as with the sensuality piece, I send this whole initial conception to the idea graveyard, and decide, as with "Beyond the Blue," to wing it.

I find myself going horizontal again, making that darn horizon line, this time in red, and trying to build around it. To encourage myself, I remember Rothko's basic rectangular shapes surrounded by auras; it worked for Rothko and everyone loved it.

It is almost impossible to proceed if one does not believe in the effort. Years of working from models have me steeped in the desire to create virtual space, that grand illusion that you are not looking at a flat canvas but something that invites the eye in and lets it roam. There is nothing for me more satisfying in painting than to make that illusion pop, and so I persist with this canvas even though I have little confidence in it. At some point it occurs to me to make the square canvas into a circle, a porthole, and so I do just that, and it makes my illusory environment feel like a snow globe or a fishbowl. Eventually, this painting reaches the "no turning back" mark. Either I must make it a better version of itself or walk away. I return to the basics.

In abstract work, when the references are swept away or obscured from view, what is left? It is clear that the answers are found in the basic elements of visual art—light, shape, color, line, texture, and space. And because they stand naked, disconnected from actual objects, they must be perfected to an advanced degree.

The color has to sing, the texture soothe and startle, the line be sure and strong, the light powerful. The work has to provide a road map, a place for the eye to enter, roam, and then exit. I am keenly aware of this as I ponder my visual fishbowl.

I let it dry so these elements can be perfected and I can add the shine. I am determined now to make it gleam, putting forth its most glorious face. I try and try and then let it be.

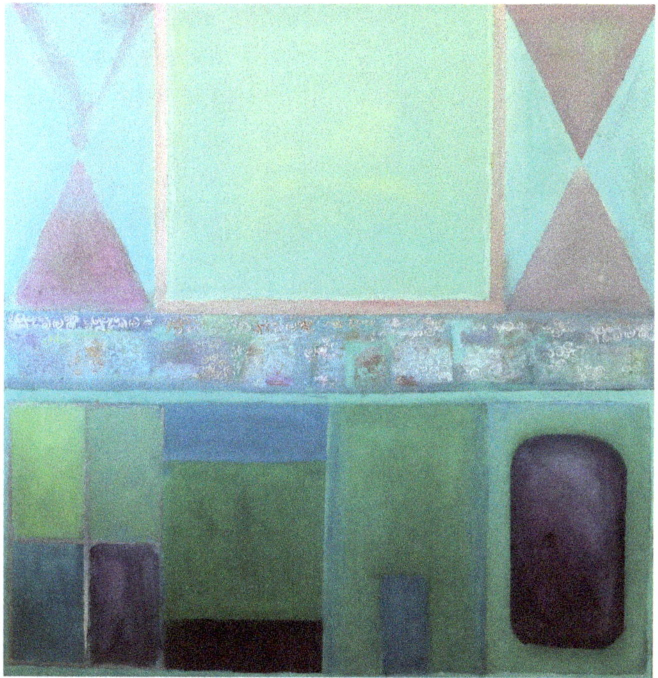

Green Light, 2022, Oil on canvas, 48 x 48 inches

Returning to it a week later, I am not happy. No matter what I do, I have no faith in this work. The rounding of the canvas just seems like a trick, and I decide to just give it up. I leave the demarcation—what was the red line—take the sander and just grind out the paint. I decide I will try again, but not today. It will be there when I am ready to give it another go.

When I do finally return, maybe a week later, I decide to just be a painter and put on some beautiful paint, beautiful color, beautifully applied. Can't go wrong with that, can I? I shall let this painting paint itself. What choice do I have? The painter is out of ideas!

Returning to the medium is never a bad idea as, in my experience, the paint eventually begins to speak to the painter and hopefully to make some sense. It begins to speak to me of light, one of my favorite subjects, and I decide I will just make this about pieces of light, radiating color, and very simple shapes that do not distract from the beautiful, colorful light.

The finished piece is called *Green Light*, as green takes the lead in this play. Funny, isn't it? I started this piece trying to paint play. Maybe I have just let the paint play. Is that good enough?

Abstract Painting #5

I started this experiment being dubious about my ability to make non-representational paintings. Here I am at the end of it, ready to make the last in the series. My usual practice, and the assignment I give myself, is to inject my emotions and thoughts into my subjects—to make it personal, the way I see things, the way I feel. That's what I'm interested in projecting. Not the thing itself. Just my take on it.

To accomplish this, I *use* the subject. I take information from it and comment on it. I may take just a tiny part, and the work may be very different in appearance from my subject. I may take a lot, and the viewer may even say I have copied it.

With these works, I have no subject, no concrete subject, just something ephemeral, a word, a feeling, a vague puff of smoke of an idea. And this feels very uncomfortable to me. It makes me think that I am faking it, making stuff up, which is not what I do. I do not invent well. Like a cellist, I have always thought of myself as an interpreter.

This is a very important insight, I think.

So, what to do for this last experiment?

I first try to do something nonemotional, a geometric design. I think of a deconstructed box or set of planes. I draw and paint them using a ruler, taping the shapes and filling them with paint. All the time I am doing this, I am thinking, *this is not me, what the hell am I doing?*

But I continue. Then I get the idea to imagine a ribbon going on and under the sides of the box. I draw and paint this ribbon shape, very deliberately. *Who am I fooling by deconstructing the box? Someone will see it as representational.* Then I step back and look at this non-Carolyn painting. I decide I just cannot continue with it. Let's face it, geometric shapes, boxes, rulers, and tape are just not me. I mix a big pot of paint and cover the whole mess. *Finito.*

Now, what to do for my last effort?

Once the surface is dry, I start a new painting by taking some juicy paint—magenta—and plopping it down on the canvas. In a blob, not a shape. I throw on some other colors. And then I call it a day. What I haven't done is what's important for now. I haven't made geometric shapes, and I haven't make anything representational. I'm at neutral and plan to sleep on this.

Next day in the studio I take a cold hard look at my canvas. I assess. It's colorful, it's not representational, but it says absolutely nothing. *Okay, what now?*

Then my eye catches a glimpse of what is outside my studio window. I have a porch overlooking a lovely little garden. Beyond the garden is a trellis. And sitting in the middle of it is a Buddha I carved out of wood. It's a spot I love and spend a lot of time in.

Let me take elements of this lovely place that I have such affection for, place them on the canvas in joyous equanimity. Not in any particular order, proportion irrelevant. Just there. All the hints of all the things that bring me such joy. The old concrete fountain. The white trellis. My rocking chair. The happy leaves and flowers. All shuffled, none identified, all finding their place on the canvas. Of course I must include the Buddha as it is the center of it all. But it's difficult to disguise. I decide that nothing need be whole or solid, and I can make penetrations of the leaves and other objects into the Buddha.

As I suspected, abstraction for its own sake leaves me cold. What interests me is scooping up all of the visual goodies that, for one reason or another, move me and encourage me. The challenge, then is to present them infused with this emotion.

My work is semiabstract. I love the elements, but without their attachment to something felt, I just can't get excited. I don't want to copy what I see, but I don't want to ignore it either. I want my viewer to attach meaning to what he sees on my canvas. How

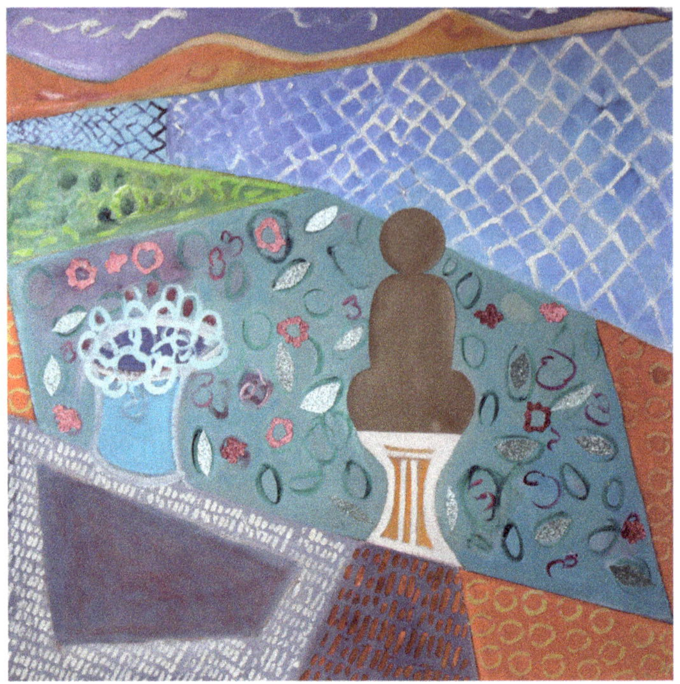

The Zen Garden, 2022, Oil on canvas, 48 x 48 inches

else will they get anything out of it? I want the viewer to see and feel the emotion in my chair, my pot, my human face.

That's because it is not a chair, or a pot, or a face. It is just paint. But it is paint coming off the brush of a living, breathing, sentient, and engaged being who wants to share her vision with whomever might want to look at it.

Making this piece is a revelation. It is amazing how our work teaches us. As I am making it, I find that I need an underlying structure that pleases me. In my search for this, I try various shapes that I extract from the garden. Some work in the composition, some I find I must junk. The fountain shape doesn't cut it, neither does the chair, the table, the bird. The Buddha is the centerpiece and it takes me a while to realize that the Buddha shape has to be simplified to the max so it becomes an icon.

I practice drawing the Buddha and keep simplifying it until it is the most reductionist shape it can possibly be. I draw it on the canvas and then proceed with other shapes: the column it sits on, shapes in the pavement, the trellis, and, of course, the garden itself.

Once I have a structure, it occurs to me that what I really want to do now is to go wild with the paint and adorn this structure with the most joyous and happiest paint I can put on. In the service of that, I make the trellis shape with my fingers, willy nilly, not neatly. I scribble leaf shapes all over the green shape for the garden. I use a stencil and make little marks all over my concrete divisions. Then I get some glittery paper, cut out the Buddha shape, and primitive leaf and flower shapes, and glue them to the canvas.

The resulting work, Zen Garden, is not a pretty painting. It is messy and jumbled, but I am happy with it because the making of it is truly an expression of the joy I have been talking about in this book. It is probably my favorite of the five works I made for this experiment. It is the one that brought me to myself.

Coda to this Experiment

We all like to know the ending to the story, so I will say that I enjoyed this experiment in abstraction, and as you might have surmised, I have returned to my work in figurative art. But it left a residue in my thinking.

I want more abstraction in my work, and this experiment has encouraged me to leave more unsaid and to allow my figures to be less defined, A good result, I think, which makes the experiment very worthwhile. Do you agree that everything we do and experience has an effect, changes us? And if we are fortunate, we find a way to make it meaningful and worthy?

A Last Note Before I Close

I have a confession to make. The idea for this book arose because of the title, *The Zen of Art*. When it popped into my head, I did some research to see if the title had already been used. Wonder of wonders, it had not. So, no kidding, then I had to write the book. I had a lurking thought that I might not be able to, as I am an artist, not a philosopher.

On the other hand, I have lived a long time and made enough mistakes that I might have something worthwhile to say. I've been at the easel now for over forty years, so I've a pretty good handle on the process of making art, at least my process. So, I said, *let's try it, and see what happens.*

That was a few years ago, and little by little, I added a thought, like a diary entry. It was the year of the pandemic, when there wasn't a lot going on outside, and like most people, I crawled onto an easy chair and ruminated. *The Zen of Art* is that rumination.

I let the thoughts hop onto the page as they came to me, without a lot of fanfare. The book is written in a casual yet authentic style, so the reader can see the architecture of my thoughts as they emerged. That is purposeful because as I am the standard bearer for making art in a Zen fashion, I had to make this book in the same way. I wanted the reader to imagine I was talking to them, having a chat about life and making art, being honest and not censoring, while sitting in the rocking chairs on my porch, feeling the lovely wind, and listening to the wind chimes, overlooking what to me is my Zen garden. I would say, *Isn't this delightful?* And you would say, *Yes, what a lovely day.*

We are so fortunate to be alive, to have the opportunity to make our way in the world, and to create ourselves. Overriding all the difficulties, we must acknowledge the privilege we share to become ourselves, to learn, to love, to be.

There are so many blessings, and art—making it ourselves

and enjoying it with others—is one of them. It is surely one of humankind's greatest and most rewarding achievements.

I hope that when you put down this book, your heart is lighter, your step more vigorous, and your mind zapped with the desire to create. Thanks for sharing your precious time with me.

Namaste,

Carolyn

ABOUT THE AUTHOR

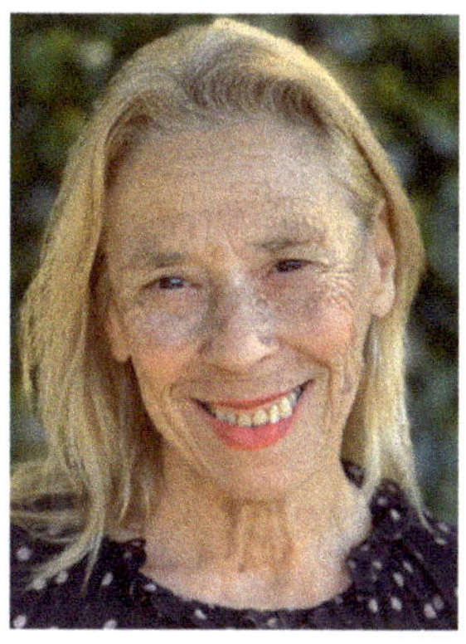

CAROLYN SCHLAM is an award-winning painter, sculptor, and published author. Her work has appeared in many museums, galleries, and publications. *The Zen of Art* now joins her other books on art process and appreciation for adults and children. Visit her website to learn more: www.carolynschlam.com

ACKNOWLEDGEMENTS

I want to acknowledge the wonderful people who worked with me to bring this book to market: my publisher and editor, Christine Cote, who did a magnificent job in editing and designing this book; my literary agent, Susan Schulman, who championed it and encouraged me; and the people in my life whom I love and who play the largest part in inspiring me: most especially my sister Rebecca, who is my daily support; and my god-daughter Erica, who is such a bright light.

Other inspirations from the path to this book: my teachers Norman Raeben and Blanche Evan; Zen teachers Ram Dass and Alan Watts; fellow artists and friends. So many influences play their part in bringing a book like this to the page: the opera singers who inspire me as I write and paint; my dog Izzy who lies contentedly at my feet as I dream; the poets and songwriters whose voices lift me. My thanks to one and all.

SHANTI ARTS

NATURE ▪ ART ▪ SPIRIT

Please visit us online
to browse our entire book catalog,
including poetry collections and fiction,
books on travel, nature, healing, art,
photography, and more.

Also take a look at our highly regarded art
and literary journal, *Still Point Arts Quarterly*,
which may be downloaded for free.

www.shantiarts.com

www.ingramcontent.com/pod-product-compliance
Lightning Source LLC
LaVergne TN
LVHW052352100826
845147LV00013B/823

* 9 7 8 1 9 6 2 0 8 2 2 1 1 *